READING ADAPTATIONS

READING ADAPTATIONS

NOVELS AND VERSE NARRATIVES
ON THE STAGE, 1790–1840

Philip Cox

Manchester University Press
Manchester and New York

distributed exclusively in the USA by St. Martin's Press

Published by Manchester University Press
Oxford Road, Manchester M13 9NR, UK
and Room 400, 175 Fifth Avenue, New York, NY 10010, USA
http://www.man.ac.uk/mup

Distributed exclusively in the USA by
St. Martin's Press, Inc., 175 Fifth Avenue, New York,
NY 10010, USA

Distributed exclusively in Canada by
UBC Press, University of British Columbia, 6344 Memorial Road,
Vancouver, BC, Canada V6T 1Z2

British Library Cataloguing-in-Publication Data
A catalogue record for this book is available from the British Library

Library of Congress Cataloging-in-Publication Data applied for

ISBN   0 7190 5340 4 *hardback*
            0 7190 5341 2 *paperback*

First published 2000

07 06 05 04 03 02 01 00   10 9 8 7 6 5 4 3 2 1

Typeset
by Helen Skelton Publishing, London
Printed in Great Britain
by Bell & Bain Ltd, Glasgow

Contents

FOR JULIE

Acknowledgements

A NUMBER OF PEOPLE have provided invaluable help and guidance during the process of this book's composition. I would like to thank Anne Janowitz and Clifford Siskin for supporting my grant application to the British Academy and David Worrall for sharing his knowledgeable enthusiasm for William Moncrieff with a fellow enthusiast. I would also like to thank Michael Worboys and the Cultural Research Institute at Sheffield Hallam University for providing the sabbatical leave which enabled me to complete large sections of the book. My colleagues within the English Department at Sheffield Hallam have offered continual support and a stimulating environment within which to work. Thanks are due in particular to my fellow 'Romanticists' Robert Miles, Emma Clery and Glenn Dibert-Himes, and also to Steven Earnshaw and (the historian) Peter Cain for their informed and incisive help with specific stages of my research. I am grateful to the AHRB for a grant which funded a particularly rewarding period of study at the British Library. Finally, but most importantly, I thank Julie Morrissy for her encouragement, her informed understanding of the theatre, and her general forbearance.

Curbar
1999

Adaptation and the ideologies of genre

THE ADAPTATION OF A NARRATIVE TEXT from one medium to another has a long history in western culture, finding its most prominent twentieth-century manifestation in the adaptation of novels into films or television programmes. Prior to the advent of film and television, however, adaptation flourished in the theatre. From the late eighteenth century through to the present day, the theatre has demonstrated an interest in reworking narratives from other genres, particularly the novel, for stage (re)presentation. The wide range of adaptations discussed in the present book gestures towards the widespread occurrence of this phenomenon in the period we now term 'Romantic'. As the novel became an increasingly popular and culturally visible genre, dramatists began to exploit the narrative affinities between it and their own genre so that, by the time of Scott's ascendancy as a novelist, Allardyce Nicoll suggests that 'the whole field of fiction was eagerly and systematically sacked' by those writing for the theatre.[1] Yet it was not simply the novel to which dramatists turned during this period – narrative poetry too was rewritten for the stage and, again, Scott provides important examples with the early decades of the century witnessing adaptations of *The Lady of the Lake*, *Marmion*, *Rokeby*, *The Bridal of Triermain* and *The Lord of the Isles*.[2] In general, as the number of both theatres and theatregoers grew in an unprecedented manner, as H. Philip Bolton argues, 'demand for theatrical entertainment increased very substantially, and to fill that demand in rushed the hack dramatists with versions of virtually every recent novel'.[3]

1

It is evident, then, that adaptation was popular – what need to be explored are the possible reasons for this popularity. An initial point of departure for such an enquiry might be to introduce more recent theories concerning the practice of film adaptation in the twentieth century. John Ellis, for example, relates the processes of adaptation to what he takes to be the inevitable practices of modern reading:

> The form of the narrative novel resists re-reading in our culture: the vast majority of novels are designed to be read once and once only, just as the narrative film is intelligible at one viewing. Re-reading or re-viewing the same text always threatens to disappoint: the process of production of the illusion becomes too obvious, the memory interferes. Adaptation into another medium becomes a means of prolonging the pleasure of the original presentation, and repeating the production of a memory. The process of adaptation should thus be seen as a massive investment (financial and psychic) in the desire to repeat particular acts of consumption within a form of representation that discourages such a repetition.[4]

To a certain extent this can provide us with a useful model which can, in part at least, explain an audience's desire to reproduce the 'memory' of a novel (or narrative poem) that they have already read. Yet what we need to keep in mind is the fact that the cultural and economic situation described by Ellis has its origins in the very period that is the subject of our present enquiry. When Ellis writes of novels which 'resist re-reading' he is in effect referring to reading practices which begin to take hold in the late eighteenth and early nineteenth centuries. Once more, this change can be charted through the career of Sir Walter Scott. Scott's undoubted popularity was accompanied by his notorious productivity which hardly gave his readers time to dwell upon (or re-read) individual texts. This market-driven production of demand and supply was viewed uncomfortably by even those reviewers who responded favourably to his work. Thus the *Quarterly Review* of October 1821 reviews eight novels by Scott at the same time and, whilst noting their 'merit', 'originality' and 'influence', also reveals a certain implicit dissatisfaction:

> The reader may expect an apology for our having delayed noticing the works that compose the long list prefixed to this article. We are disposed

to apologise for noticing them at all. And certainly, most of the motives which direct us in the selection of writers to be reviewed, are in this case wanting. We cannot suppose to draw attention to works which are bought, and borrowed, and stolen, and begged for, a hundred times more than our dry and perishable pages. We have little expectation that the great author, who tosses his works to us with such careless profusion, will take the trouble of examining our strictures – and still less that he will be guided by them.[5]

Beneath the humour there is an underlying concern which relates to the habits of both reading and writing which are generated by the Scott phenomenon. Readers scramble indecorously and, it is implicitly suggested, in a rather undiscriminating way for the latest Scott novel whilst the author himself carelessly 'tosses' his work to his readers. The reviewer is faced with the problem that the period's most famous novelist appears to be producing 'throwaway' novels. Indeed, at the end of the review, he returns to this point:

> Our parting exhortation to the 'Great Unknown' must be, if he would gratify the impatience of his contemporary readers, to write as much and as quickly as possible: if he would transmit his name to posterity, in such a manner as to do full justice to his extraordinary powers, to bestow a little more time and leisure in giving them their scope; in concentrating those excellencies which he has shown to be within his reach, and in avoiding those blemishes, which he cannot but have taste to perceive.[6]

To translate this into the terms used by Ellis: Scott appears to be producing novels which resist rereading because they are only designed to fulfil the demands of the marketplace which constantly demands new stimulus and new products to sell; the reviewer calls for him to create novels which are specifically designed for rereading because they aspire to a continued afterlife represented by the notion of 'posterity'.

In part, then, adaptation in this period can be seen to be produced by the same market forces that produced Scott's profusion and which are an early version of the similar economic forces which underpin Ellis's argument. What we need to register, however, is the disorientating novelty of this proliferation of texts – a situation which E. J. Clery in her account of the adaptations, plagiarisms and translations of supernatural fiction has described as being perceived as 'a chaos of shifting identities, mysterious reduplications or multiple repetitions'.[7] As Clery also points out, this confusion was one which related to questions of literary (and cultural) 'value' and to the (as yet unformulated) distinction between 'high' and 'low' culture. Critical discussion of this distinction is, of course, fraught with difficulties. Rather than attempt to offer a definitive account of what constitutes 'low' or 'popular' culture (which might very well prove to be an impossible task), the present book aims to examine the implicit and explicit ways in which contemporary writers attempted to distinguish between what was increasingly seen as 'serious' literature on the one hand and more popular 'entertainment' on the other. My starting point is similar to that of Morag Shiach when, at the outset of her own account of 'popular culture', she identifies it as 'a persistent term in cultural analyses, which points us towards a consideration of cultural hierarchies and of the relation between the social and the cultural'.[8] At the same time, I am aware that the use of such binary oppositions as 'high' and 'low' can potentially lead to an oversimplification of both social and cultural interactions within a given historical period. Tim Harris, in a very useful overview of the critical issues involved in this, reminds us of the strong presence of what he terms the 'middling orders' who form an influential third presence which has to be taken into consideration. Whilst, Harris notes, 'the middling orders often sought to create social and cultural distance between themselves and those beneath them', it is also the case that 'it is by no means clear that we should invariably locate the middle ranks of society on the elite side of the cultural divide'.[9] However, as will be seen through the course of this book, with the growth of an influential middle-class reading public in the late eighteenth and early nineteenth centuries this confusion was being addressed directly and indirectly through public discussion of issues surrounding popularity and literary value. Bill Bell describes Charles Dickens's readership in the 1830s as being caught between 'humble origins and the respectable world to which they aspired' and thus he identifies 'the experience of the petty-bourgeois reader' as 'one of complex and even contending class affinities'.[10] For such readers, the articulation of a text's place within a cultural hierarchy was a crucial factor in determining their own place within a social hierarchy.

However, in approaching such issues in relation to the cultural positioning of stage adaptations, modern theories of film adaptation are less helpful, if not misleading. Film is predominantly viewed as 'low' or 'popular' culture whereas the novel is frequently associated with high artistic value.[11] The relationship between a novel and its dramatic adaptation in the Romantic period would, of course, have had very different cultural resonances: the drama had an established literary genealogy which invested it with a potential cultural respectability whereas the novel was, historically, a relative newcomer which was often denied such respectability as a result of the very popularity which rendered it so culturally prominent. Yet it would be wrong to suggest that this distinction between the two genres was either stable or unproblematic for the situation is further complicated by the fact that, from a historical perspective, we can trace a narrative which charts the rise of the novel as a 'serious' literary form during the nineteenth century and a corresponding decline, in Britain, of the theatre as a site for high artistic seriousness. Furthermore, additional complications emerge when we attempt to establish the position of poetry in relation both to drama and the novel. As will be seen, poetry, which traditionally allied itself with drama, came increasingly to distinguish itself from that genre during the course of the period and yet, like drama, could be seen to be fighting a rearguard action against the increasing popularity and acceptability of the novel as a literary form. It soon becomes evident that the generic interrelationships brought into play through adaptation are varied and complex and that they offer a potentially revealing insight into the origins of still prevalent distinctions between 'high' and 'low' culture and the relationship between art and the marketplace.

The context for such social and ideological change has been described and analysed in the influential work of Jon Klancher, particularly in his seminal study *The Making of English Reading Audiences, 1790–1832* (1987). Developing the work of Jerome McGann, which warned critics of the dangers of 'an uncritical absorption in Romanticism's own self-representations', Klancher attempts to replace the Romantic poets' often idealised and abstracted notion of their audience with a more materially based account of actual groups of readers. In so doing, he is attempting to resist a critical and aesthetic discourse 'which essentializes and thus mystifies what was in fact a troubled contention over power, signs, and the function of culture itself'.[12] Deploying a methodology derived in part from the work of both Mikhail Bakhtin and Pierre Bourdieu, Klancher demonstrates how this troubled semiotic contention is crucially involved with the ways in which, during this period, different social groups were attempting to define their own changing positions within society. It was, he argues, a period of enormous growth and development, a period in a state of social flux which

> demanded that British readers reorient themselves. Yet this deliberative, strategic historical moment – the Romantic period in England – would give rise to the great systemic culture whose battle lines, much more firmly drawn, were those of high culture and mass culture, bourgeoisie and working class, the imperial nation-state of Europe – in short, the Victorian and then modernist societies whose categories early nineteenth-century writers had only begun to glimpse.[13]

The present book aims to articulate another strand in this complex narrative of the emergence of a recognisably 'modern' society. The ways in which novels, verse narratives and their adaptations present themselves to the public, and the ways in which they are critically received both individually and as genres, can be read as part of the materially based semiotic struggle which forms the core of Klancher's study.

In addition, however, this kind of literary history needs to work alongside recent scholarly interest in the role played by genre in defining both the literary and the more general cultural productions of the late eighteenth and early nineteenth centuries in Britain. Academic studies have revealed not only the wide range of different genres deployed by writers during this period, but also the fact that such generic profusion is often accompanied by innovative generic combination and modification – a practice which has increasingly been read in relation to historically specific social and political change. The work of Clifford Siskin in particular has provided a methodological framework within which to approach these complex interactions between genre and history. This methodology, which is articulated at length in *The Historicity of Romantic Discourse* (1988), is distinctive in that it aspires to a 'generic history' as opposed to a 'history of genre' and thus aims to use 'genre to construct history rather than the other way round'.[14] Siskin suggests that by focusing in detail upon generic usage at a particular historical juncture we can begin to appreciate how the discourses of genre are inflected by broader cultural concerns. Unlike more traditional accounts of a quasi-organic development of poetry, drama or the novel, Siskin's work enables us to perceive the historically contingent nature of literary genres – and also, I would argue, the ways in which social and political meaning is generated by the explicit and implicit strategies adopted in order to differentiated each genre from the others. This historically situated differentiation between contemporary genres is particularly significant for an exploration of the generic tensions introduced when a work in one genre is 'adapted' for (re)presentation in another. A study of the adaptation of poems and novels into plays during the Romantic period brings into sharp focus the constantly shifting relationships that existed between the three genres. The cultural politics of adaptation are complex, therefore, but, as a result, they provide ideal material for a 'generic history'. Before embarking upon a study of adaptation itself, however, we need to look in slightly more detail at contemporary definitions and redefinitions of the three distinct but variously interrelated genres, beginning with poetry, traditionally a central genre in most critical formulations not only of 'Romanticism' but also of the 'Romantic' period. This assumed centrality can be both understood and modified through an exploration of poetry's often proprietorial attitude towards the drama.

UNTIL RECENTLY THE DRAMA of the Romantic period was a marginalised area of critical concern and this marginalisation was primarily a result of a more sustained academic interest in the period's poetry. As Daniel P. Watkins observes, 'One casualty of past scholarly efforts to establish the lyric as the premier Romantic literary form – one small area that might be used as a test site for reevaluating and reshaping our historical understanding of Romanticism and our awareness of the politics of Romantic studies – is Romantic drama, until recently almost universally dismissed as a failure'.[15] Although I would fully endorse Watkins's conclusions here, it is perhaps significant that my own interest in this area is, ironically, a direct consequence of my earlier work on the period's poetry and, specifically, what could be termed the 'subgenres' of poetry.[16] Whilst working on such obvious subgenres as the sonnet or the epic, I also found that I was increasingly concerned with the poets' sustained obsession with drama – either in the form of the so-called 'closet' drama or as plays which were actually written for the stage (and yet often not performed). What surprised me was the ease with which I could include drama within the category of poetry, whereas I had felt obliged carefully to disassociate my more general enquiries from what I took to be the wider generic antagonism between poetry and the novel. My understanding of this larger relationship between poetry and the novel was that the period witnessed a shift from the literary dominance of poetry to that of the novel, but I began to wonder where the third major generic category – that of the drama – fitted into this relationship. Moreover, if a generic history of the period enables us to see the complexities of historical process, I felt that such a history would be seriously incomplete if it failed to take into account the thriving theatre of the period.

The inclusion of drama under the generic category of poetry in my previous work was, I now realise, an effective exclusion of the generic category of drama itself. However, such exclusion derives in the first instance from the critical writings of the Romantic poets themselves which draw, in their turn, upon a long-established critical tradition which includes drama within the definition of the poetic. Such thinking is well illustrated by William Wordsworth's Preface to his *Poems* of 1815 in which he describes how the 'materials of poetry ... are cast, by means of various moulds, into divers [*sic*] forms'. The image of the mould here indicates a characteristic attitude to genre as something which gives shape to a poem but which is none the less independent of the essence of 'poetry' contained within or represented by a specific text. The second of the 'forms' elaborated by Wordsworth is that of the dramatic:

2ndly, The Dramatic, – consisting of Tragedy, Historic Drama, Comedy, and Masque; in which the poet does not appear at all in his own person, and where the whole action is carried on by speech and dialogue of the agents; music being admitted only incidentally and rarely. The Opera may be placed here, in as much as it proceeds by dialogue; though depending, to the degree that it does, upon music, it has a strong claim to be ranked with the Lyrical. The characteristic and impassioned Epistle, of which Ovid and Pope have give examples, considered as a species of monodrama, may, without impropriety, be placed in this class.[17]

Just as the poem (in a specific generic 'form' or 'mould') is preceded by an essence of 'poetry', so drama here is ironically haunted by the presence of the poet. The irony, of course, lies in the fact that Wordsworth seems to be claiming that this is precisely not the case: 'the poet does not appear at all in his own person'. Yet the subtextual implication here is that the poet does appear, if only in disguise (not 'in his own person' but in the form of others). The Romantic notion of poetry is so intricately involved with the creation and presentation of 'self' that one could hardly expect Wordsworth to write differently. However, the outcome of this is that his definition of drama is one which excludes the dramatic (or, perhaps more precisely, the theatrical). Wordsworth suggests, no matter how indirectly, that we read a play for an understanding of the poet who wrote it rather than for an appreciation of, say, the dramatic clash of character: our focus is the poet in his [sic] study rather than a staged performance. When Wordsworth introduces the subgenre of monodrama he effectively conflates it with the form of the epistle and directs us to a consideration of the written poems of Ovid and Pope. One would hardly think from this that the monodrama was a popular contemporary theatrical form, of which Jeffrey N. Cox writes that it 'uses both language and music to express ... emotional states; ... it even drew upon the spectacular stage devices of other contemporary theatrical forms. The monodramatist uses all of the resources of the theatre to accomplish a single goal: the direct and immediate communication of passion.'[18] The theatricality of the form is glossed over by Wordsworth: for him drama is founded upon words rather than gesture and spectacle ('the whole action is carried on by speech and dialogue of the agents'). The inclusion of 'music' into Wordsworth's account of the dramatic might at first appear to undermine this tendency but, on closer examination, one can see that, in this instance too, the discussion is one which implicitly denies the theatre. Wordsworth admits the possibility of music being introduced into a play, if only 'incidentally and rarely'. The model for such practice is, presumably, Shakespeare and the spectre lurking in the wings is probably the extreme musicality of the 'melodramatic' productions to be found in the unlicensed London theatres. Yet even Wordsworth's allowance of a certain musical element needs to be analysed more closely. He refers to the possibility of the opera being placed under the category of the dramatic only to suggest that, because of its extended reliance upon music, it should more properly be included under the category of the lyrical. The lyrical is Wordsworth's next category in the Preface: '3rdly, The Lyrical, – containing the Hymn, the Ode, the Elegy, the Song, and the Ballad; in all which, for the production of their *full* effect, an accompaniment of music is indispensable.' What, we have to ask, is the effect of the italicised *'full'* in this sentence? Wordsworth did not set his own hymns, odes, elegies, songs or ballads to music – is he suggesting that these are in some way incomplete as a result? Rather than a necessary component of the successful lyric poem (as Wordsworth appears to suggest), it would seem that a musical accompaniment is a necessary fiction that accompanies all lyrics. The *'full'* effect of the lyric demands an imaginative response from the reader which supplies what we might term a 'mental' music.

The performance of live music to accompany a lyric poem suggests a public immediacy and a uniqueness of social occasion analogous to a performance in the theatre. The replacement of such performance with a 'mental' music is in turn analogous to the resituation of performance from public stage to 'mental theatre' in much 'closet' drama written by the Romantic poets. This issue has been debated at length by a variety of critics, including myself, and I have no wish to cover old ground here (although I do shortly wish to return to the question of what constitutes 'closet' drama). Of more immediate concern is the obvious strain apparent in Wordsworth's attempts at generic classification. He wishes to categorise drama as a subgenre of poetry but implicitly recognises that if drama is to be made to confirm to his notions of what constitutes poetry then its theatrical elements will have to be effaced. In the 'Essay Supplementary to the Preface' (1815), this tendency becomes more marked when Wordsworth turns to consider the reputation and status of Shakespeare:

A Dramatic Author, if he write for the Stage, must adapt himself to the taste of the Audience, or they will not endure him; accordingly the mighty genius of Shakespeare was listened to. The People were delighted; but I am not sufficiently versed in Stage antiquities to determine whether they did not flock as eagerly to the representation of many pieces of contemporary Authors, wholly undeserving to appear upon the same boards.[19]

The opening sentence here is both audacious (how can one be a dramatic author if one does not write for the stage?) and entirely to be expected. Wordsworth's distrust of the public and his fear of the vicissitudes of the marketplace which were increasingly determining the 'value' of literary production, is mapped back on to Shakespeare in the early seventeenth century. Shakespeare as a type for the early nineteenth-century poet can only have been a successful writer of performed plays insofar as he compromised his artistic integrity. Seen in these terms, theatrical success included the possibility of poetic failure. That Shakespeare did not fail poetically is only, according to Wordsworth, the result of his supreme genius. 'At all events', he writes, 'that Shakespeare stooped to accommodate himself to the people, is sufficiently apparent; and one of the most striking proofs of his almost omnipotent genius, is, that he could turn to such glorious purpose those materials which the prepossessions of the age compelled him to make use of'. The clash here is one between 'high' and 'low' culture, between poetry which retains an apparent artistic integrity and a fidelity to a Romantic notion of creative 'genius' on the one hand and, on the other, a public performance which appeals to 'popular' demand as expressed through the economic power of the marketplace. These oppositions are precisely those which have already been introduced in the earlier discussion of adaptation, but what needs to be highlighted at this point is the fact that drama, as a genre, is significantly, and complexly, situated between the two opposing terms of the argument.

THE RESPONSE OF THE canonical Romantic poets to this awkward repositioning of the drama has usually been read in terms of their development of the ultimately flawed form of the 'closet' play. This in turn has been interpreted in relation to their growing political conservatism, in that a fear of the consequences of public political action was translated into a reluctance to have their work exposed to the uncontrollable elements of theatrical performance. Increasingly sceptical in regard to the possibility of revolutionary programmes being acted out in the real world, poets such as Wordsworth, Coleridge and Southey turned their attentions to the complexities of the individual psyche. An indirect result of this is that there is a corresponding rejection of the theatrical enactment of their 'dramatic' works – as Julie A. Carlson puts it, 'the wish that links revolution and theatre requires a closeted drama of the mind'.[20]

The underlying impulse located by such arguments is undoubtedly an important element in the production of these texts and yet, from a generic point of view, the 'closet' drama still presents many problems, not the least being its applicability as a general generic category. Jeffrey N. Cox, for example, questions its final usefulness in comparison with a category like that of the monodrama:

> The category of closet drama is of less importance, because it does not define a specific form; rather it is a measure of the distance between the romantics' theatrical aspirations and the realities of early nineteenth-century theater. The closet drama is a contingent category, for this distance changed as the theater responded to romantic dreams; that is, many works that were published as closet dramas – Shelley's *The Cenci* or Musset's plays, for example – later met with some theatrical success. In some cases, the closet drama represented not a moribund armchair drama but bold dramatic experimentation. The monodrama, then, was a dramatic form of the day. The closet drama sought the theater of the future.[21]

Cox usefully highlights what he terms the 'contingent' nature of the closet drama, suggesting that there is no simple generic category into which the diverse plays often grouped under this heading can be placed. Thus some texts, such as Shelley's *Prometheus Unbound* (which is generically labelled as a 'lyrical drama'), can clearly be seen to reject the possibility of stage performance whereas others, such as the same poet's *The Cenci*, were written with the intention of theatrical production but were rejected by contemporary theatre managers. Other plays, such as William

Wordsworth's *The Borderers*, present slightly more ambiguous evidence. If we believe his much later note dictated to Isabella Fenwick in 1843, he had 'no thought of the Stage' when he initially wrote the play. However, we also know that he was angered and upset when the play was rejected by Covent Garden in 1797, expressing his frustration at 'the deprav'd State of the Stage at present'.[22] There is a sense, then, in which Wordsworth rejects the theatre because it had rejected him in the first place and for us to accept unquestioningly his later assertion concerning earlier intentions is to collude with his own implicit desire to deny retrospectively the importance of the contemporary stage.

The 'closet' drama, therefore, needs to be read alongside and against performed drama if we are to be able to appreciate its full generic significance for, as Daniel P. Watkins has noted, the 'drama-theater distinction itself is a problem for literary and social historical investigation and should not be accepted on its own terms as a given distinction between types of dramatic expression'.[23] Wordsworth's poetic theory, as revealed in the Preface and 'Essay Supplementary' of 1815, demonstrates his tendency to appropriate drama within the genre of poetry and thus to deny the aspect of performance. His re-presentation of *The Borderers* does something very similar. If we, in turn, read plays by the canonical Romantic poets which were initially intended for the theatre (such as *The Cenci* or Keats's *Otho the Great*) as closet texts then we too are espousing Wordsworth's Romantic ideology and denying the material conditions which determined (and, in another sense, prevented) their production.

In attempting to reconstruct these material conditions, it is helpful to consider the four-volume anthology of 'rejected plays' which was published in 1814 by John Galt under the title *The New British Theatre, A Selection of Original Dramas, not yet acted; some of which have been offered for Representation but not Accepted with Critical Remarks by the Editor.*[24] The stated intention of this anthology is to challenge the contemporary restrictive management practices of the London theatres: Galt claims that his hope is that a collection of 'rejected pieces' 'would enable the lovers of the drama to appreciate the taste and the judgement with which the management of the theatres is conducted, in relation to the refusal and reception of plays, and how far the assertion is correct, that the pantomimic state of the stage is owing to a decline in the dramatic genius of the nation'.[25] Galt's contempt for the 'pantomimic state' of the British stage is akin to that of Wordsworth and others who share what has been seen as the period's antitheatrical prejudice. However, rather than rejecting the stage – as Wordsworth and others seem to have done – Galt engages directly with those he assumes are primarily responsible for its debased state, that is, the managers of Drury Lane and Covent Garden. It is their poor judgement – and the existence of the monopoly belonging to the two licensed theatres – that prevents the true 'dramatic genius of the nation' from being widely appreciated for, Galt states, he 'cannot believe, while in every other branch of polite learning the nation has been regularly advancing, that the drama should have been as regularly retrograde'.[26]

The implicit nationalism of Galt's arguments become more explicit as he begins to draw analogies between aesthetic taste and political judgement:

> If the public taste be so corrupted, as the apologists for the present state of the drama assert, it is a painful, an alarming consideration, and more dangerous to the future welfare of the country than all those excrescencies in the government, to which theoretical quacks so loudly call attention, and endeavour to exalt themselves by offering to cure. But as in all other matters the nation never thought more judiciously than it does at present, and as through a long course of political events of the most extraordinary nature, it has acted with an admirable constancy of affection for those institutions and principles which the experience of all ages had demonstrated to be the best, we will not believe that the good sense of England is so far impaired as the public taste appears to be corrupted, judging from the exhibitions of the stage.[27]

Galt here draws upon the same parallels between the corruption of the contemporary theatre and the threat of revolutionary political instability that Julie Carlson and others have observed in the work of the canonical Romantic poets. Galt suggests that the extravagances of theatrical spectacle could indicate as grave a danger as any posed by revolutionary ideology if, and only if, such extravagance was a direct result of the aesthetic 'taste' and 'common sense' of the country as a whole. However, drawing upon a Burkean appeal to traditional values and what he takes to be the English people's rejection of French radicalism, he believes that a drama freed from the tyranny of the monopoly management of the licensed theatres will produce plays which, like the contemporary political system in Galt's eyes, is based upon 'an admirable constancy of affection for those ... principles which the experience of all ages had demonstrated to be the best'.

Galt's pronouncements are clearly predicated upon what he sees as the national moral and political importance of the theatre as an institution. As he writes later in his Preface:

> To what cause, in so enlightened a country as England, are we to attribute the neglect of so great, so general an institution – an institution, perhaps, as essential to manners in a refined state of society, as the church is to morals? The stage has, in England, become almost as great an organ of public instruction as the pulpit. ... It would be better if some of those who are so vociferous for alterations in the state of the government, would look a little more to their private trusts; and evince that they really possess some capacity for directing national affairs, by the judgement and liberality with which they promote the interests of the drama – a department of the domestic oeconomy which has more permanent influence on the character of the nation, than the measures of any administration, and which, in a moral point of view, is infinitely more dignified and important than the objects of half of all the questions annually discussed in the House of Commons.[28]

It is evident from this that for Galt the theatre is an institution which is in as much need of protection as both church and parliament. Whilst he might at first appear to differentiate between 'morals' and 'manners', the fact that the theatre is 'almost as great an organ of public instruction as the pulpit' suggests the deep seriousness of purpose he invests in the performance of drama. On the one hand, Galt is arguing that it is not the depraved moral (and political) sensibilities of the English people which has caused the debased state of English theatre; on the other, he is implicitly suggesting that the moral repercussions of a depraved theatre are potentially serious because, as a national institution, it has ceased to perform its function of 'public instruction'.

Galt's *New British Theatre* takes as its starting point many assumptions which are shared by William Wordsworth and other Romantic poets who seem to have rejected the theatre in favour of 'closet' drama. Unlike them, however, Galt actively campaigns for new opportunities for dramatic performance and a reform of day-to-day theatre management. The irony, none the less, is that the restrictive material conditions of the early nineteenth century mean that Galt can only conduct his campaign on the printed page rather than in the theatre itself. The plays that he puts forward as part of his programme for reform are initially presented for reading rather than performance: the 'new' British theatre is performed in the mind of the reader rather than upon the stage and therefore, in its reception, becomes analogous to those plays that have been labelled 'closet' drama. The material conditions of the early nineteenth century create a situation where an attempt to reintroduce a 'serious' purpose into the drama only succeeds in perpetuating a division between a theatre which depends increasingly upon spectacle and popular entertainment and the production of plays with a 'higher' cultural purpose which almost by definition exclude themselves from performance.

This problem can be pursued further through a brief consideration of the work of Joanna Baillie who also actively campaigned for theatrical reform. Ten years before Galt's *New British Theatre* she had published a volume of *Miscellaneous Plays*, in the introduction to which she confides:

> I must also mention, that each of the plays contained in this volume has been, at one time or another, offered for representation to one or other of our winter theatres, and been rejected. ... I merely mention it, because otherwise it must have appeared absurd to introduce from the press what has been expressly written to come before the public in a different manner, without making any attempt to present it in its own peculiar mode.[29]

In highlighting this aspect of the publication of her plays, Baillie in effect draws attention to the implicit contradictions of the Wordsworthian dramatist who does not write for the stage. Baillie, unlike Wordsworth, has a definite desire for her plays to be performed and yet she is acutely aware of the conditions which make such performance difficult or, perhaps, even impossible. She differentiates the plays in *Miscellaneous Plays* from those in her larger, ongoing 'Series of Plays' which, as she wrote elsewhere, attempted to fulfil 'our desire to know what men are in the closet as well as on the field' by offering plays which focused upon a particular 'passion' delineated through the carefully observed psychological processes of a central character.[30] These 'Plays of the Passions' were, she claims, 'not altogether well fitted for the stage, as it is commonly circumstanced' and yet, she significantly continues, 'I think plays upon that plan are capable of being made upon the stage more interesting than any other species of drama.'[31]

Baillie's publication of her plays can therefore be seen as an attempt to (to paraphrase Wordsworth's dictum in the 1815 'Essay Supplementary to the Preface') create the taste by which (s)he is to be enjoyed, or, as Baillie herself puts it:

> So strong is my attachment to the drama of my native country, at the head of which stands one to whom every British heart thinks of with pride, that a distant and uncertain hope of having even but a very few of the pieces I offer to the public represented to it with approbation, when some partiality for them as plays that have been frequently read shall have put it into the power of future managers to bring them upon the stage with less risk of loss than would be at present incurred is sufficient to animate me to every exertion that I am capable of making.[32]

The frequent reading of the plays, this argues, will pave the way for their future successful performance by creating a public demand which will fulfil the economic requirements of the theatre managers. Yet what this fails to take into account (and something of which Baillie is intensely aware at other moments in her introduction) is the necessary differences between a read and a performed text. Baillie's *De Monfort* (one of the original 'Plays of the Passions') was, for example, performed successfully at Drury Lane in 1800 with Kemble and Siddons in the leading roles and yet the performance still received a rather telling criticism from Elizabeth Inchbald: 'That fine play, supported by the most appropriate acting of Kemble and Siddons, is both dull and highly improbable in the representation ... its very charm in the reading militates against its power in the acting.'[33] The implication here is not simply that a play which is successful in the closet might fail on the stage: Inchbald implies that the very qualities which make the text attractive to read disqualify it from successful performance.

Baillie's desire as a dramatist to record the feelings of great men in the 'closet' rather than 'on the field' suggests a move towards drama as private and introspective rather than as a form which presents the vicissitudes of public action. Yet this ironically becomes 'closet ' drama in a double sense because the plays' focus upon the private is more often than not mirrored in the private act of the closeted reading experience which has to stand in for the scene of future public enactment in the theatre anticipated in Baillie's introduction to *Miscellaneous Plays*. In that introduction, Baillie refers reverentially to Shakespeare as the 'head' of the national tradition of drama to which she relates herself and it is, of course, the case that, despite the successes of Kean, Siddons and others in Shakespearean roles, the Romantic period was one which witnessed an increasing tendency to present Shakespeare as a dramatist whose greatness was misrepresented and diminished in performance and who could only be truly appreciated through the act of reading. The most famous argument for the impossibility of successfully performing Shakespeare's plays is made by Charles Lamb in his essay 'On the Tragedies of Shakespeare, considered with reference to their Fitness for Stage Representation' (first published in 1812). In this essay, Lamb suggests that:

> It may seem a paradox, but I cannot help being of opinion that the plays of Shakespeare are less calculated for performance on a stage, than those of almost any other dramatist whatever. Their distinguishing excellence is a reason that they should be so. There is so much in them, which comes not under the province of acting, with which eye, and tone, and gesture, have nothing to do.[34]

Lamb implies that Shakespeare is concerned with the mind rather than the body, with private emotion and feeling rather than public deeds, and that it is this emphasis upon the internal that precludes him from success in the theatre. In her 'Plays of the Passions' Baillie attempts to emulate those characteristics which Lamb singles out as Shakespeare's distinctive strengths and thus renders her own work potentially lacking in 'Fitness for Stage Representation'.

Jonathan Bate has written that Lamb's essay 'marks a watershed in the history of one particular appropriation of Shakespeare: the tradition which singles out character, which psychologizes and internalizes, which Romanticizes and novelizes'.[35] From a generic perspective it is the final term that is the most provocative. One might readily identify 'internalisation' and an interest in individual 'psychology' as central concerns of what has come to be defined as Romanticism and one might similarly describe, say, Joanna Baillie's quasi-Shakespearean dramatic aspirations as, in this sense, Romantic. It seems initially disconcerting, however, to be asked (in the context of my own argument rather than that of Bate) to see both Romanticism (which one normally identifies with the lyric) and movements for theatrical reform as being in some way intimately associated with the contemporary 'rise' of the novel. Yet it is only by introducing this third term that one can begin to appreciate the full complexity of the period's generic interrelationships. The changing self-definitions of both poetry and drama are produced by the same social and economic forces which bring about the increasing prominence of the novel – and yet it is the novel which is best situated in relation to contemporary material conditions for, as Daniel P. Watkins notes, the novel 'was born with, shaped, and enabled by a bourgeois worldview'.[36] In order to accommodate economic changes relating to the production and reception of cultural artefacts, poetry and drama had both in their different ways to define themselves in relation to the novel which, as a genre, appeared to relate most effectively to contemporary social structures. It is this process of generic self-definition at a time of economic transformation that is foregrounded in the act of adaptation.

THE FIRST CHAPTER OF THIS BOOK focuses more explicitly upon the genre of the novel by taking William Godwin's *Caleb Williams* and George Colman (the Younger)'s adaptation, *The Iron Chest*, as a specific case study. Using Elizabeth Inchbald's commentary on this adaptation as a starting point, the chapter examines the ways in which both the novel and the play can be seen to rehearse ideological tensions through the semiotics of genre classification. At the same time, a comparison of *Caleb Williams* with *The Iron Chest* reveals how a generic distinction between certain kinds of novel on the one hand and the emerging dramatic form of the melodrama on the other can be read not simply in light of developing distinctions between 'high' and 'low' culture but can also be related to differing accounts of how the individual is constructed within and against the notion of society.

In writing *Caleb Williams*, Godwin was attempting to produce a more 'popular' means of conveying some of the philosophical ideas contained within his *Enquiry Concerning Political Justice*. When Colman adapted the novel as *The Iron Chest*, he rendered the text more potentially 'popular', but at the same time he implicitly altered its ideological potential. The ideological issues which surround the popular literary (or theatrical) text come more prominently to the fore with the emergence of Walter Scott as a best-selling writer in the first decade of the nineteenth century. The first of the two chapters on Scott begins by considering the implications of the vociferous debate occasioned in contemporary periodicals by the unprecedented success of his narrative poems. In these articles and reviews one can detect what Jon Klancher might describe as the critics' attempts to 'reorient' themselves in a rapidly changing society. Scott's popularity gives rise to an important reconsideration of the criteria which are called upon to determine notions of literary value. The result is an early, tentative and largely implicit series of distinctions between what would come to be seen as 'high' and 'low' culture. The remainder of the chapter examines in detail a number of adaptations of Scott's *The Lady of the Lake* and describes how generic reformulations of the narrative suggest different and competing ways of representing notions of the individual in the early nineteenth century.

The second chapter on Scott takes as its primary focus the question of national rather than individual identity. Through an analysis of a number of adaptations of *Ivanhoe*, it is argued that the plays problematise many of the notions of heroic behaviour found in Scott's novel and foreground those aspects of the original book (particularly those concerning the presentation of Isaac and Rebecca) which implicitly bring into question its apparently simple celebration of national and cultural unity. This is particularly the case in George Soane's adaptation of *Ivanhoe* as *The Hebrew*, in which Isaac is presented as the play's Lear-like tragic hero. Whilst all too often dismissed as the work of mere theatrical hacks, such analysis demonstrates that the contemporary theatre was capable of intelligent and provocative reinterpretations of the novels that were chosen for adaptation.

The final chapter studies adaptations of the early work of Charles Dickens, in effect Scott's successor as a novelist with 'serious' pretensions who, none the less, courted the popularity of the marketplace in order to earn a (very good) living. H. Philip Bolton opens his introductory account of Dickens and adaptation by declaring that the writer 'has been both a literary and popular phenomenon'.[37] The chapter in the present book demonstrates that this was, indeed, always the case from virtually the very beginning of Dickens's career as a writer. However, a recurrent critical difficulty was (and has since been) that of disentangling the 'literary' and the 'popular' which were (and sometimes still are) felt to be mutually exclusive categories. Central to this process of disentanglement was Dickens's own desire to present himself as a 'serious' novelist for which, from very early on, he received support from his friend the critic John Forster. The chapter traces in some detail Dickens's and Forster's clash with the playwright William Moncrieff who had written adaptations of both *Pickwick Papers* and *Nicholas Nickleby* and who is satirically portrayed in Chapter 48 of the latter novel. Coming from a similar background to Dickens but generally regarded as a hack writer rather than a serious artist, Moncrieff embodied exactly the kind of professional writer from whom Dickens had to differentiate himself if he was to achieve his own literary ambitions. The chapter concludes with an analysis of Moncrieff's *Sam Weller, or, the Pickwickians* in which, in scenes which are far more explicitly political than their counterparts in *Pickwick Papers*, Moncrieff can be seen to be putting forward a case for a more inclusive and liberal attitude towards notions of literary value.

Most of the plays discussed in the pages of this book are today almost completely unknown despite their enormous contemporary popularity. The inclusive attitudes towards literary value advocated by writers such as Moncrieff have given way, since the nineteenth century, to the triumph of a more exclusive and restricting model of what Jon Klancher has termed the 'politics of cultural classification'.[38] The present study aims to rediscover the significance of these forgotten adaptations as part of a larger contemporary critical project which is attempting to remap the Romantic period as one which witnessed the emergence of the complex cultural formations we associate with modernity.

Notes

1 Allardyce Nicoll notes the popularity of such adaptations: 'Fiction was rapidly becoming a dominant form of literature, and the minor dramatists found here in plenty that for which they were seeking – plots, characters and dialogues ready formed, the *scenario* (and more than the *scenario*) on which they could base their hastily written plays. The dramatisation of novels had begun in the latter half of the preceding century, but it was not until the time of Scott that the whole field of fiction was eagerly and systematically sacked', in *A History of English Drama 1660–1900: Volume IV Early Nineteenth-Century Drama 1800–1850* (Cambridge, Cambridge University Press, 1955), pp. 91–2.

2 Byron's poetry was also popular, with, for example, versions of *Mazeppa*, *The Bride of Abydos* and *The Corsair* appearing on the stage.

3 H. Philip Bolton, *Dickens Dramatized* (London, Mansell Publishing, 1987), p. 15. Bolton's Introduction offers one of the best overviews of the practice of adaptation in this period.

4 John Ellis, 'The literary adaptation: an introduction', *Screen*, 23:1 (May/June 1982) 3–5, pp. 4–5.

5 *Quarterly Review*, XXVI (October 1821) 109.

6 *Quarterly Review*, XXVI (October 1821) 148.

7 E. J. Clery, *The Rise of Supernatural Fiction 1762–1800* (Cambridge, Cambridge University Press, 1995)

8 Morag Shiach, *Discourse on Popular Culture: Class, Gender and History in Cultural Analysis, 1730 to the Present* (London, Polity Press, 1989), p. 14.

9 Tim Harris, 'Problematising popular culture', in Tim Harris (ed.), *Popular Culture in England, c.1500–1850* (London, Macmillan, 1995), p. 17.

10 Bill Bell, 'Fiction in the marketplace: towards a study of the Victorian serial', in Robin Myers and Michael Harris (eds), *Serials and Their Readers 1620–1914* (Winchester, St. Paul's Bibliographies; New Castle, DE, Oak Knoll Press, 1993), p. 136.

11 Thus Samuel Goldwyn's 1939 version of *Wuthering Heights* was viewed with scepticism by many contemporary reviewers because it appeared to offer an implicit threat to the inherent cultural 'value' of Emily Bronte's novel – 1939 also being the year in which the Brontes were awarded a memorial in Westminster Abbey. For further details of the contemporary response to the 1939 film, see Philip Cox, '*Wuthering Heights* in 1939: novel, film and propaganda', *Bronte Society Transactions*, 20:5 (1992) 283–8.

12 Jon P. Klancher, *The Making of English Reading Audiences, 1790–1832* (Wisconsin, WI, The University of Wisconsin Press, 1987), p. 5; the earlier quotation from Jerome McGann (which is quoted by Klancher on the same page) is from *The Romantic Ideology: A Critical Investigation* (Chicago, IL, University of Chicago Press, 1983), p. 1.

13 Klancher, *The Making of English Reading Audiences*, p. 13.

14 Clifford Siskin, *The Historicity of Romantic Discourse* (Oxford, Oxford University Press, 1988), p. 10.

15 Daniel P. Watkins, *A Materialist Critique of English Romantic Drama* (Gainesville, FL, University Press of Florida, 1993), p. 3.

16 See my *Gender, Genre and the Romantic Poets* (Manchester, Manchester University Press, 1996).

17 Preface to *Poems* (1815), text from Stephen Gill (ed.), *William Wordsworth*, The Oxford Authors (Oxford, Oxford University Press, 1984), p. 627.

18 Jeffrey N. Cox, 'The Vision of Romantic Tragic Drama in England, France, and Germany', unpublished PhD thesis, University of Virginia, 1981, p. 55.

19 'Essay Supplementary to the Preface (1815)', in Gill (ed.), *William Wordsworth*, p. 646.

20 Julie A. Carlson, *In the Theatre of Romanticism: Coleridge, Nationalism, Women* (Cambridge, Cambridge University Press, 1994), p. 1.

21 Cox, 'The Vision of Romantic Tragic Drama', pp. 56–7.

22 For the Isabella Fenwick note, see John O. Hayden (ed.), *William Wordsworth: The Poems* (Harmondsworth, Penguin, 1977), Vol. I, p. 938; for the biographical context for the rejection of *The Borderers*, see Stephen Gill, *William Wordsworth: A Life* (Oxford, Clarendon Press, 1989), p. 132.

23 Watkins, *A Materialist Critique of English Romantic Drama*, p. 5.

24 A useful account of Galt's life and work is to be found in I. A. Gordon, *John Galt: The Life of a Writer* (Edinburgh, Oliver and Boyd, 1972).

25 John Galt (ed.), *The New British Theatre* (London, Henry Colburn, 1814), Vol. 1, p. i.

26 Galt, *The New British Theatre*, Vol. 1, p. ii.

27 Galt, *The New British Theatre*, Vol. 1, pp. iii–iv.

28 Galt, *The New British Theatre*, Vol. 1, pp. xiii–xiv.

29 Joanna Baillie, 'To the reader', *Miscellaneous Plays* (2nd edn, London, Longman, Hurst, Rees, and Orme, 1805), pp. xi–xii.

30 Joanna Baillie, *The Complete Poetical Works of Joanna Baillie* (Philadelphia, PA, Carey and Lea, 1832), p. 13; quoted in Ellen

Donkin, *Getting into the Act: Women Playwrights in London 1776–1829* (London, Routledge, 1995), p. 162.

31 Baillie, *Miscellaneous Plays*, pp. viii–ix.

32 Baillie, *Miscellaneous Plays*, pp. xii–xiii.

33 Letter to Mrs Phillips, in James Boaden, *Memoirs of Mrs Inchbald* (2 vols, London, Richard Bentley, 1833), Vol. 2, p. 34, quoted in Donkin, *Getting into the Act*, p. 163.

34 Charles Lamb, 'On the tragedies of Shakespeare', in Lamb, *Lamb as Critic*, ed. Roy Park (London, Routledge and Kegan Paul, 1980), p. 88.

35 Jonathan Bate, *Shakespearean Constitutions: Politics, Theatre, Criticism 1730–1830* (Oxford, Clarendon Press, 1989), p. 132.

36 Watkins, *A Materialist Critique of English Romantic Drama*, p. 9. Watkins argues that poetry was better able to adapt to changing economic conditions than was the drama. This is undoubtedly true if we limit our attention to 'serious' theatre. The fact remains, though, that the drama survived – and flourished – as a 'low' cultural form in the nineteenth century. A full generic history needs to take this into consideration and give full emphasis to its broader cultural importance.

37 Bolton, *Dickens Dramatized*, p. 3.

38 Klancher, *The Making of English Reading Audiences*, p. 14.

CHAPTER ONE

Caleb Williams
and The Iron Chest

IN AN ADDRESS 'To the artist', published in *The Artist* in 1807, Elizabeth Inchbald discusses the differences between the writer of plays and the writer of novels. The novelist, she suggests, is, by comparison with the dramatist, a 'free agent':

> He lives in a land of liberty, whilst the Dramatic Writer exists but under a despotic government. Passing over the subjection in which an author of plays is held by the Lord Chamberlain's office, and the degree of dependence which he has on his actors – he is the very slave of the audience. He must have their tastes and prejudices in view, not to correct, but to humour them ... the will of such critics is the law, and execution instantly follows judgement.[1]

In its criticism of the restrictive tyranny of theatre management and legislation, this echoes the feelings voiced by Galt in his introduction to *The New British Theatre* yet, whereas Galt appeals to the redeeming good taste of theatre audiences, Inchbald appears to share Wordsworth's fear of the moblike summary (in)justice of spectators in the theatre. Whereas Galt looks towards a newly reformed theatre and Wordsworth clings to an elevated, and perhaps anachronistic, notion of poetry which is appreciated by an idealised 'people', Inchbald implicitly locates a bourgeois (and potentially paradoxical) sense of individual liberty and moral responsibility within the genre of the novel. As both novelist and dramatist (and actress), Inchbald is well placed to make comparisons between the two genres and it is thus significant that, whilst she does not reject the theatre, she none the less defines the novel as more conducive to successful aesthetic and moral effect in the early years of the nineteenth century.

During this period Inchbald plays an important role in the formation of an accepted canon of dramatic writing – and of critical opinion upon it – through the publication, in twenty-five volumes, in 1808 of *The British Theatre: A Collection of Plays with Biographical and Critical Remarks by Mrs Inchbald*.[2] One of the plays included in this anthology is George Colman, the Younger's adaptation of William Godwin's novel *Caleb Williams* as *The Iron Chest*. In her introduction to this play Inchbald returns interestingly to the relative merits of the two genres and comments upon the process of adaptation itself. She notes how Colman's adaptation of *Caleb Williams* is always preceded – and hindered – by the reader's or spectator's prior knowledge of the original novel:

> its highest claim to notice is derived from its fable and incidents having been founded on that extraordinary and well-known novel, called 'Caleb Williams' – This last circumstance has perhaps, contributed less to its good than to its adverse fortune … The novel … has too forcibly struck the minds and hearts of its numerous readers, to admit, on that subject, of any deeper impressions; and to follow an author, in a work of such powerful effect, what hope could be cherished of arriving at the goal which he had reached, or of approaching him nearer than as one of his admiring train?[3]

The adapter of a novel for the stage is, according to this, inevitably faced with his or her own belatedness and lack of originality: the adaptation can only aspire to equal but not surpass the success of its predecessor and the creative act is in danger of becoming simply synonymous with one of dutiful homage to an earlier, more accomplished literary achievement. Inchbald's advice to Colman, on the evidence of both this play and an adaptation from Sterne, is to avoid writing such plays:

> In comparing these two plays … with Mr Colman's other dramas, the legitimate offspring of his own mind, it will be wished that he never draw materials from any other repository; or that, like the illustrious Shakespeare (whose phraseology he sometimes follows) he would stoop to dramatise old ballads, or childish romances, where his talents might

act without restraint, and the admiration of his model never sink him
into vain imitation.[4]

The implication here is that adaptation is an 'illegitimate' genre –
a 'bastard' form that possesses a doubtful lineage, being (in this
case) neither simply novel nor play but something which occupies
a rather disconcerting middle ground. Moreover, this illegiti-
macy extends into the realm of authorship as the adaptation can
be said to be the legitimate 'offspring' of neither the novelist
nor the dramatist. Its authorship – and thus its authority – can
therefore be said to be questionable in a way which ironically links
Inchbald's arguments with those fears concerning the possibility of
preserving an inviolate and autonomous poetic 'self' which were
earlier discussed in the previous chapter in relation to William
Wordsworth.

Colman's adaptation of a contemporary novel, according to
Inchbald, threatens to subvert his authority as an autonomous playwright and yet, in the second half of the passage quoted, she
proceeds to suggest that this need not necessarily be the outcome of
adaptation as a whole. Citing the authoritative precedent of
William Shakespeare, she indicates that the adaptation of 'old
ballads and childish romances' might result in plays that were more
successfully self-defining. Inchbald's argument here significantly
combines and conflates the temporal and the generic: the ballads
and romances are suitable for adaptation because they belong to an
earlier time and so do not possess the same currency as a contemporary novel and yet, in addition to this, Inchbald implies that
whereas the novel is a (or *the*) contemporary genre, ballads and
romances, as genres, belong to an earlier cultural epoch and are
thus ripe for adaptation because they have been generically superseded by other genres, such as the novel, which speak more specifically for the contemporary world. As Inchbald continues to discuss
this topic it appears that the drama too is in danger of being superseded by the new possibilities opened up by the psychological novel
as represented by Godwin's text. She observes that the 'finer details
in "Caleb Williams" allow no representation in action: the dramatist was here compelled merely to give the features of the murderer's
face; while the novelist portrayed every shade of his countenance,
every fibre that played in forgetful smiles, or was convulsed by the

pangs of remembrance'.[5] Inchbald suggests that the novel, unlike Colman's play, is able to describe in minute detail the gestures and expressions of its protagonists. However, although she writes simply of the portrayal of such actions, it is clear that her argument is in fact referring to both their portrayal and interpretation: the novelist reads certain gestures and expressions in terms of clearly defined thought and feelings such as guilt, forgetfulness and remembrance. In the theatre, on the other hand, such physical signs are read in a far less clearly defined way and without the same degree of authorial control.

In *Caleb Williams* itself, Godwin has the narrator Williams comment upon a similar issue:

> I shall continue to speak in my narrative of the silent, as well as the articulate part of the intercourse between us. His countenance was habitually animated and expressive much beyond that of any other man I have seen. The curiosity, which, as I have said, constituted my ruling passion, stimulated me to make it my perpetual study. It will also probably happen, while I am thus employed in collecting together the scattered incidents of my history, that I shall upon some occasions annex to appearances an explanation, which I was far from possessing at the time, and was only suggested to me through the medium of subsequent events.[6]

Falkland possesses an 'animated and expressive' countenance which one might appositely term dramatic in that it suggests meaning through action and gesture rather than relying simply upon words. Within the novel, however, this dramatic quality has to be (re)presented through a narrator who is able to 'annex to appearances an explanation'. The potential excesses and indeterminacies of dramatic expression are contained, controlled and redeployed in a way which guarantees a precise transmission of meaning and significance.

As Richard Cronin has suggested, Williams can be interpreted a s a representative of the novelist who refashions experience – 'collecting together the scattered incidents of ... history' – in order to present an aesthetically and ideologically coherent text.[7] Insofar as this generic self-reflexivity is concerned with the relationship between the 'dramatic' and the 'novelistic' it anticipates developments in the novel which Peter Brooks locates in the later nineteenth century. In *The Melodramatic Imagination*, Brooks notes the reliance of melodrama upon silent gesture and wordless action, both of which, he suggests, are later appropriated and redeployed within French and English nineteenth-century novels:

> Gesture as transcribed in the novel appears to be a 'betrayal' of theatrical gesture in that it refuses to actualize – through description, visual notation – the motions to which it gives such a significant status. If Balzac and Dickens and James often refer us to the theatre as the aesthetic model of their own representations, and clearly think of their written 'scenes' and gestures in theatrical terms, they are nonetheless more concerned with the decipherment and translation of gesture than with its pure figure.[8]

This 'decipherment and translation of gesture' is precisely the activity described by Caleb Williams in the passage quoted earlier and, furthermore, there is a significant amount of evidence to suggest that, for Godwin as well as those later novelists discussed by Brooks, the theatre provided an 'aesthetic model' for the novel. Not only does Williams have recourse to theatrical analogies – for example, 'My life has for several years been a theatre of calamity' (p. 3) or 'I lift the curtain, and bring forward the last act of the tragedy' (p. 79) – but there is also a frequent movement towards the 'translation of gesture' as in, for example, 'His look bespoke the unquietness of his mind, and frequently wandered with an expression of disconsolateness and anxiety' (p. 5).

Although Brooks can write of this novelistic use of gesture as an act of 'betrayal', in general he sees it in far more positive terms. Indeed, he proceeds to interpret it as a realisation of 'the deepest implications of the gestural sign' in that it allows meaning to be reascribed to those actions which are in danger of failing to communicate adequately. For Brooks, gesture always 'suggests an intention and a direction of meaning' and the novel facilitates the successful completion of this purpose. Generically, one could say that Brooks's arguments imply that the melodrama finds a generic fulfilment within the genre of the novel. Brooks himself suggests that the novel's successful self-fulfilment is enabled by its adoption of melodramatic representations of gesture; he claims that 'gesture in the novel becomes, through its translation, fully resemanticized, and may stand as emblematic of the whole novelistic enterprise of finding significance in man's terrestrial, even quotidian actions'.[9] This is a persuasive argument but there is, none the less, a sense of what Clifford Siskin calls a 'history of genre': the novel, which became the dominant genre during the nineteenth century, is here allowed to be the central term in the generic narrative told by Brooks.[10] In addition, this narrative is itself rendered problematic by the fact that its salient features can, as has been seen, be traced to a considerable extent within late eighteenth- and early nine-teenth-century English texts which predate the developments in (French) melodrama outlined by Brooks within his study. In order to replace Brooks's 'history of genre' with a (necessarily partial) 'generic history' of the Romantic period, it is useful to concentrate in the first instance more specifically upon the example provided by *Caleb Williams* and its representation as *The Iron Chest*.

THE MOST OBVIOUS WAY in which to approach *Caleb Williams* in terms of genre is to read it as an enactment of a tension between the values of chivalric romance on the one hand and those of the realist novel on the other.[11] Thus Falkland is seen to embody values which are outmoded in both a social and a literary sense – as can be seen by the account of his reaction to Tyrell's violent behaviour:

> He was too deeply pervaded with the idle and groundless romances of chivalry ever to forget the situation, humiliating and dishonourable according to his ideas, in which he had been placed upon this occasion. There is a mysterious sort of divinity annexed to the person of a true knight, that makes any species of brute violence committed upon it indelible and immortal. To be knocked down, cuffed, kicked, dragged along the floor! sacred heaven, the memory of such a treatment was not to be endured! No future lustration could ever remove the stain: and, what was perhaps still worse in the present case, the offender having ceased to exist, the lustration which the laws of knight-errantry prescribe was rendered impossible. (p. 97)

The whole passage is pervaded by a narrational irony which makes use of hyperbolic language in order to ridicule Falkland's adherence to 'idle and groundless' beliefs which have been superseded. Simultaneously, Godwin registers the supersession of chivalric or heroic romance narratives by those revealed through the apparently more factually based genre of the realist novel. As Marilyn Butler and others have noted, there is clearly a political agenda here: Falkland, like Burke, laments that the 'age of chivalry' is dead but Williams (and Godwin), like Paine, celebrate this demise of the old regime in order to present 'Things As They Are' (to use the original title of the novel).[12]

If we turn to Colman's *The Iron Chest*, we can also begin to discern interesting generic tensions which can, in turn, be related back to the original novel. William Hazlitt saw the play in terms of an awkward clash of the tragic and the comic: 'in Colman', he writes, 'you do not know whether the comedy or tragedy is principal; whether he made the comic for the sake of the tragic, or the tragic for the sake of the comic; and you suspect he would be as likely as any of his contemporaries to parody his most pathetic passages ... The great beauty of Caleb Williams is lost in the play.'[13] Within *The Iron Chest*, Mortimer (the Falkland character) is throughout a potentially tragic figure: he is seemingly aristocratic, honourable and noble-spirited but, in addition, he possesses an intrinsic flaw relating to his misguided and excessive sense of reputation and fame. He has an acute sense of justice and yet is tragically led to violate both the spirit and the letter of the laws he is trusted to enforce:

> I fear'd this boy;
> He knew my secret; and I blacken'd him,
> That, should he e'er divulge the fatal story,
> His word might meet no credit. Infamy
> Will brand my mem'ry for't: Posterity,
> Whose breath I made my god, will keep my shame
> Green in her damning record. Oh I had –
> I had a heart o'erflowing with good thoughts
> For all mankind! One fatal, fatal turn,
> Has poison'd all! Where is my honour now? (III.iii, p. 81)[14]

This speech, from the final scene, clearly points towards a conclusion of high tragic seriousness with Mortimer anticipating the punishment due to the 'good' man who has tragically chosen to worship false 'gods'.

And yet, as Hazlitt observes, this tragic note is not consistently maintained during the play, its seriousness is frequently undercut by a simultaneous comic element which is often associated with the lower-class characters. Thus the tragic-comic tension is revealingly inflected by the discourse of class in a way which mirrors the more explicit struggle between the aristocratic Mortimer and his servant Wilford (the Williams character in the play). In general, one could argue that the function of the comic is to act as a pointed reminder of 'things as they are' in opposition to a more idealised 'tragic' construction of experience. In this way the generic opposition within the play can be seen to map on to the generic interaction of realist novel and chivalric romance at work within the novel. The comic functions in such a way as to puncture simple moral serious- ness with disruptive irony. Thus, for example, Fitzharding (Mortimer's brother) has a highly earnest speech concerning his principled decision to stand by the accused Wilford:

> Friend, I will stoop
> To prop a sinking man, that's called a rogue,
> And count him innocent, till he's found guilty.
> I learn'd it from our English laws, where Mercy
> Models the weights that fill the scales of Justice;
> And Charity, when Wisdom gives her sentence,
> Stands by to prompt her. Till detection come,
> I side with the accused. (III.ii, p. 70)

This is evidently directly oppositional to Godwin's attack on the injustice of 'English laws' in *Caleb Williams*: here the English judi- cial system is, through the use of resonant personifications, presented as a force which represents values which are both essen- tial and universal. The person to whom this speech is delivered, however, is Samson, the roguish child of a poacher who has found employment within Mortimer's household. Samson is a comic figure whose pointed rejoinder to Fitzharding implicitly problema- tises his celebration of English justice:

> Would I had known
> Your worship sooner. You are a friend indeed!
> All undiscovered rogues are bound to pray for you:
> So, Heaven bless you! (III.ii, p. 70)

In blessing Fitzharding, Samson comically reveals his own status as an 'undiscovered rogue' and yet the rejoinder has more wide-ranging implications for it implicitly highlights the potential of this system for corruption and complacency. Moreover, there is an underlying dramatic irony due to the fact that, at this stage in the play, it is not Wilford but Mortimer who is in truth the 'undiscovered rogue'. In a way unintended by Samson himself, his speech suggests the injustices wrought by 'Justice' and implicitly reminds the audience of the guilt of Mortimer who has been declared innocent by the very legal processes extolled by Fitzharding.

Another – and perhaps more appropriate – way of seeing the generic tensions within Colman's play, however, would be to describe it as an embryonic melodrama in which the developing form of the melodrama attempts to assert itself against the residual form of the tragedy. There is throughout a melodramatic dependence upon music and song both to further and ornament the ongoing narrative and there is also a tendency towards both tableaux (as witnessed by the opening of Act I, Scene i in Rawbold's cottage where the scene of 'Poverty and Wretchedness' is accompanied by a 'Glee') and spectacle (see, for example, the setting of Act II, Scene v which is 'The Inside of an Abbey, in Ruins: Part of it converted into an Habitation for Robbers' and where a 'musical dialogue and chorus' takes place in which the 'Robbers enter through various Parts of the Ruins, in Groups'). The 'trial' scene at the end of the play enacts a potentially melodramatic public opposition between Wilford's innocence and Mortimer's guilt and, in keeping with a melodramatic triumph of 'good', Mortimer is denied a final 'tragic' death (he simply leaves the stage feeling unwell) and the play concludes with the happy reunion of Wilford with his beloved Barbara and his fellow servants. This conclusion is rounded off with a speech thanking the care of 'Providence' and with a closing song which celebrates the power of harmony.

However, whether one sees *The Iron Chest* as exhibiting a tension between comedy and tragedy or melodrama and tragedy, it would initially appear that there are significant parallels in both cases between the play's generic oppositions and those politicised generic tensions discussed in relation to *Caleb Williams*. The melodrama in particular, which Coleridge attacked in 1817 as a Jacobinical mode, would be particularly well placed to counter the aristocratic inflections of tragedy.[15] Thus far, then, one could say that there is an equivalence between chivalric romance and tragedy

33

on the one hand and the novel and comedy or melodrama on the other and that, seen in these terms, the play successfully adapts the novel's ideologically charged generic modulations into its own dramatic terms. And yet, at the same time, another generic tension can be observed within Colman's play which suggests that there is a further debate taking place between the relative claims of the novel on the one hand and the drama on the other.

The terms of this debate can be approached with reference to observations made by Inchbald in her Preface to *The Iron Chest* in which she uses the present instance of adaptation to discuss the broader differences between the genres: 'The two arts of dramatic and novel writing are ... beheld at such variance, that the reader of the novel shall enter, with Faulkland [*sic*], into all his nice, his romantic notions of honour and posthumous fame; though the auditor, or the reader, of 'The Iron Chest' shall feel no concern, unless to despise it, about all Sir Edward Mortimer's equal enthusiasm for the glory of reputation.'[16] Inchbald here signals what she takes to be the main strength of the novel as genre, that is, its ability to enter into the minds of the protagonists and to represent thought apparently directly without the mediation of spoken language or gesture. Interestingly, this issue is one that Colman himself turns to in his own play – though his conclusions are seemingly different from those of Inchbald. The relevant scene is that in which Wilford and Mortimer discuss the stature of Alexander the Great. In Godwin's novel the point of this scene is to question representations of heroism and greatness and, significantly, in disputing both the heroism and greatness of Alexander, Williams alludes to the views of Henry Fielding:

> the author of Tom Jones has written a volume to prove that he and all other conquerors ought to be classed with Jonathan Wild.
>
> Mr Falkland reddened at these citations.
>
> Accursed blasphemy! Did these authors think that by the coarseness of their ribaldry they could destroy his well-earned fame? Are learning, sensibility and taste no securities to exempt their possessor from this vulgar abuse? (p. 110)

Richard Cronin has rightly observed that the 'quarrel between Falkland and Williams is not a quarrel about facts, but a quarrel between two literary dispositions: the disposition to represent the world heroically, the disposition expressed in heroic romance, and the disposition to represent it unheroically, the disposition expressed in the novel'.[17] This distinction has already been discussed but it is worth noting how Falkland's opposition to Williams's implicit espousal of values associated with the novel refers to aspects of coarseness and vulgarity which carry evident signs of class antagonism.

In the play, Colman, whilst choosing to adapt this scene, provides it with a quite different set of referents. In place of Godwin's apparent celebration of the novel's historical truthfulness, Colman presents the spectator with a speech which brings into question the value and validity of certain kinds of private reading which one might associate with the novel. Mortimer declares to Wilford that:

> Books
> (My only commerce now) will, sometimes, rouse me
> Beyond my nature. I have been so warm'd,
> So heated by a well-turned rhapsody,
> That I have seem'd the hero of the tale,
> So glowingly described. Draw me a man
> Struggling for fame, attaining, keeping it,
> Dead ages since, and the historian
> Decking his memory in polish'd phrases,
> And I can follow him through every turn,
> Grow wild in his exploits, myself, himself,
> Until the thick pulsation of my heart
> Wakes me to —— ponder on the thing I am! (I.iii, p. 27)

This is in many ways similar to Inchbald's celebration of the novel's ability to take the reader 'inside' the mind of a protagonist and to become 'myself, himself' and yet, in contrast to Inchbald's positive presentation of this reading experience, Colman alerts his audience to the delusive dangers inherent within it. For Mortimer, reading becomes a way of misrepresenting his own historical reality: it is a form of escapism which, whilst it seems to 'rouse' him, is actually nothing more than a fallacious dream from which he must ultimately awake (as he is in effect forced to do when the truth of his previous actions is revealed in the final scene of the play). The play is not ultimately concerned with inner, psychological or imaginative 'truth' but with a truth which can be publicly revealed within society. At the end of the play Mortimer's guilt is made evident through the reading of a private 'narrative' of his crime which he inadvertently left with the 'stolen' goods he had placed in Wilford's possessions in order to incriminate him. This private document has to be made public in order for justice to be done: the written text of Mortimer's confession needs a public performance in order for it to have social effect.

Caleb Williams enacts a tension between the different values associated with certain traditional forms of (mainly) poetic narrative and those associated with the more recent genre of the novel. *The Iron Chest*, as has been seen, displays a similar tension between received 'tragic' values and a newer ideology which we can begin to associate with the emerging genre of the melodrama. And yet, at the same time, the process of adaptation reveals certain tensions between the bourgeois novel and what was increasingly to become, in England, the more proletarian form of the melodrama. The novel can be seen to stress the importance of interiority and moral responsibility enforced through moral didacticism whereas the melodrama valorises the public performance of social justice and distrusts the potentially delusive claims of interior 'truth'.[18] This is not, of course, to label one genre more radical or conservative than the other: one must keep in mind – and broaden the relevance of – Jeffrey N. Cox's dictum that 'we should not reify dramatic genres or identify them too closely with any single ideological vision'.[19] Having said this, the current analysis of *The Iron Chest* would seem to corroborate (with an earlier example) Anastasia Nikolopoulou's observations about later, early nineteenth-century melodrama, when she writes that it 'destabilized and disrupted the cultural models embedded in tragedy and the novel'.[20] Moreover, the current investigation has also suggested the extent to which discourses of social class and developing notions of high and low culture are significantly revealed through the generic configurations at play within the processes of literary adaptation in the late eighteenth century.

SUCH ISSUES OF CLASS AND literary status evidently provided an important context for Godwin's own composition of *Caleb Williams*. In writing the novel, the philosopher-turned-novelist can at one level be seen to be engaged in his own practice of adaptation as he adapts the philosophical principles embodied in the *Enquiry Concerning Political Justice* into an alternative and more readily accessible genre. In the original preface to *Caleb Williams*, Godwin provides an implicit rationale for this generic transformation:

> What is now presented to the public is no refined and abstract specula-tion; it is a study and delineation of things passing in the moral world. It is but of late that the inestimable importance of political principles has been adequately apprehended. It is now known to philosophers that the spirit and character of the government intrudes itself into every rank of society. But this is a truth highly worthy to be communicated to person whom books of philosophy and science are never likely to reach. Accordingly it was proposed in the invention of the following work, to comprehend, as far as the progressive nature of a single story would allow, a general review of the modes of domestic and unrecorded despot-ism, by which man becomes the destroyer of man. If the author shall have taught a valuable lesson, without subtracting from the interest and passion by which a performance of this sort ought to be characterised, he will have reason to congratulate himself upon the vehicle he has chosen. (p. 1)

Godwin's *Enquiry* and *Caleb Williams* are both, according to the qualities of their respective genres, intended to convey the same 'truth' about contemporary society. The generic shift is occasioned by a desire to reach a different audience, one which is not in the habit of reading 'books of philosophy and science.' In the Preface to the *Enquiry*, Godwin, whilst deploring the censorship of suppos-edly subversive publications by the contemporary government, had differentiated his philosophical work from more popular papers and pamphlets by declaring it to be 'by its very nature an appeal to men of study and reflection'.[21] The genre of the philosophical enquiry implies a specific, and very limited audience; the novel, on the other hand, is written for a far less restricted social grouping. In addition to the 'interest and passion' required by a novel, then, Godwin has a more serious, educative intention, that of bringing the educated pronouncements of the philosopher to a broader and less-educated reading public.

The success of this gesture towards a popular readership is

indicated by Elizabeth Inchbald in a letter to Godwin, written when she had just finished the final volume of the novel:

> I never felt myself so conscious of, or so proud of giving proofs of a good understanding, as in pronouncing this to be a capital work. It is my opinion that fine ladies, milliners, mantua-makers, and boarding-school girls will love to tremble over it, and that men of taste and judgment will admire the superior talents, the *incessant* energy of mind you have evinced.[22]

Inchbald's celebration of *Caleb Williams*'s appeal, however, identifies not one but two potential audiences, each of which are seen to respond to the book in different ways and for different reasons. Inchbald differentiates between the two in terms of gender and this rhetorical strategy awkwardly situates her own position as a reader. On the one hand she posits a 'feminine' readership composed of all social ranks and age groups, from ladies through to milliners and boarding-school girls, who will read the novel merely as sensational entertainment which appeals to the passions but not the intellect. On the other, she identifies a 'masculine' audience which will appreciate the '*incessant* energy of mind' conveyed by the author – the same intellectual energy, one is to assume, that lies behind the more overtly intellectual *Enquiry*. Inchbald's own response, as a woman, is problematic in that she responds in an implicitly 'masculine' fashion as is evinced by her opening claims for her own 'good understanding' which enables her to appreciate the finer points of the novel. The gendered awkwardness revealed here can be viewed as a product of Inchbald's inability to synthesise pleasurable novel reading with a more strenuous intellectual purpose: she registers the presence of both in *Caleb Williams* but has difficulty articulating the ways in which a novel can be capable of serious philosophical instruction and yet at the same time create the quasi-physical *frisson* of the Gothic tale.

Though she herself was a novelist who attempted similarly 'serious' novels, Inchbald appears to have become a victim of the influence of contemporary criticisms of the novel as a popular and therefore less intellectually rigorous genre. It is to such criticisms that Godwin turns his attention in his manuscript essay 'Of History and Romance' which was written in 1797. Godwin begins by discussing different forms of history writing and notes that many critics are disdainful of any form of history which concentrates upon individual historical figures as opposed to more abstract and general concerns:

> They disdain the records of individuals. To interest our passions, or employ our thoughts about personal events, be they of patriots, of authors, of heroes or kinds, they regard as a symptom of effeminacy. Their mighty minds cannot descend to be busied about anything less than the condition of nations, and the collation and comparison of successive ages. Whatever would disturb by exciting our feelings the torpid tranquility of the soul, they have in unspeakable abhorrence.[23]

Although Godwin is here discussing the writing of history, it is clear that he is anticipating the essay's later discussion of the novel. Behind the distinction between two forms of history writing lies the distinction between the *Enquiry* (philosophical study) and *Caleb Williams* (novel or romance): just as the *Enquiry*, according to its genre, relies upon the elaboration of abstract and general principles, so *Caleb Williams*, to return to its Preface, is dependent upon the 'domestic' and the 'passion' of the individual. Within the present essay, Godwin refutes the charges of 'effeminacy' which critics have levelled both at certain kinds of history and (by implication) the novel and appears instead to value writing which records the thoughts and emotions of the individual above that which depends upon more generalised abstractions. To support this value judgement, he appeals (in an ironically abstract fashion) to the essential qualities of 'the mind of man': 'The mind of man does not love abstractions. Its genuine and native taste, as it discovers itself in children and uneducated persons, rests entirely in individualities. It is only by perseverance and custom that we are brought to have a relish for philosophy, mathematical, natural or moral. There was a time when the man, now most eagerly attached to them, shrunk with terror from their thorny path.' However, the defence employed here possesses an implicit ambiguity: whilst it might attest to an intrinsic quality of the human mind, it also suggests, against the grain of the argument, that an enjoyment of 'individualities' can be primarily associated with 'children and uneducated persons'. The category is significantly, and perhaps unfortunately, reminiscent of Inchbald's milliners and boarding-school girls. There is the faint suggestion here of a tendency which is more explicit in the Preface to *Caleb Williams*: the novel (or a focus on 'individualities') is seen as a less advanced or less philosophical means of conveying 'truth' but a means which has to be adopted for those who have not had sufficient training or opportunity to be able to appreciate more 'intellectual' genres.

In the essay as a whole, however, Godwin is at pains to suggest the superiority of the novel or romance over general histories. His broader defence of the genre includes his belief, which is interestingly reminiscent of Falkland's speech in *The Iron Chest* about the influence of 'books', that it 'is the contemplation of illustrious men, such as we find scattered through the long succession of ages, that kindles into flame the hidden fire within us. ... While we admire the poet and the hero, and sympathize with his generous or his ardent expressions, we insensibly imbibe the same spirit, and burn with kindred fires.' Whilst, in the earlier reading of *The Iron Chest*, this act of imaginative identification was seen as a turning away from the social towards an individualised – and delusive – introspection, Godwin here argues that it is an important prerequisite of social knowledge: it is, he writes, 'necessary for us to scrutinise the nature of man, before we can pronounce what it is of which social man is capable'. 'Social man' is therefore predicated upon the 'individual' and, in a line which (as Michael Gamer observes) anticipates Joanna Baillie's Preface to her *Series of Plays*, he claims that, when considering the great characters of history, 'I am not contented to observe such a man upon the public stage, I would follow him into his closet.' Introspection replaces performance, the closet is substituted for the stage.

Whilst Godwin's ultimate goal is a transformation of society and the establishment of 'political justice', his novel (and his defence of the genre of the novel in the present essay) emphasise a necessary private transformation that is a forerunner of any change within society as a whole. At the same time, he also stresses the educative function of the novel as a form which should possess a palpable design upon its readers, providing them with access to the author's sense of 'truth' via emotional and imaginative means rather than through purely intellectual engagement. In many ways this is a recognisably Romantic project but it is also one which, as was seen in the analysis of *The Iron Chest*, is very different to contemporary theatrical practice. Marilyn Gaull, in her discussion of pantomime and melodrama, observes that both forms 'were collective rather than private expressions, drawing on common knowledge, reflecting the values of the audience more than any individual author'.[24] Theatrical adaptations heighten this element of collectivity by taking a text which is explicitly the work of an 'individual author' and reproducing it within a context in which not only the reproduction but also its reception is a collective experience. If Godwin had tacit misgivings about his own adaptation of the *Enquiry* into *Caleb Williams*, then the subsequent adaptation embodied in *The Iron Chest* should have troubled him even more because of its effective reversal of a central tendency within the novel. In *Caleb Williams*, Godwin had hoped to produce what was, in effect, a 'popular' form of his philosophical work; in *The Iron Chest* Colman reproduced the novel in a form which had the potential to reach a wider and more obviously 'popular' audience. In the process, the ideological underpinnings of the novel were significantly changed. Such changes provide an opportunity for the twentieth-century reader to observe shifting and competing accounts of the relationship between the individual and society, accounts which complicate any single narrative of the Romantic period. Moreover, they provide an insight into the complex and problematic relationship that existed between a recognisably 'romantic' ideology and the notion of a popular audience. Very similar issues are foregrounded by the critical debates which surrounded the enormous popularity of Walter Scott's verse narratives and by the very large number of stage adaptations that were occasioned by them. These poems and plays are the subject of the next chapter.

Notes

1 Elizabeth Inchbald, 'To the artist', *The Artist*, I:14 (13 June 1807), quoted in Ellen Donkin, *Getting into the Act: Women Playwrights in London 1776–1829* (London, Routledge, 1995), p. 5.

2 For an account of how Inchbald came to work on this project together with an overview of her critical opinions, see Chapter IV of Roger Manvell, *Elizabeth Inchbald: A Biographical Study* (Lantham, NY and London, University Press of America, 1987).

3 Elizabeth Inchbald, 'Remarks' on Colman's *The Iron Chest*, in *The British Theatre: A Collection of Plays with Biographical and Critical Remarks by Mrs Inchbald* (London, Longman, Hurst, Rees and Ormes, 1808), Vol. XXI, p. 1.

4 Inchbald, 'Remarks', p. 2.

5 Inchbald, 'Remarks', p. 2.

6 William Godwin, *Caleb Williams*, ed. David McCracken (Oxford, Oxford University Press, 1982), p. 118.

7 See Richard Cronin, 'Carps and *Caleb Williams*', *Keats–Shelley Review*, 1 (Autumn 1986), 35–48.

8 Peter Brooks, *The Melodramatic Imagination: Balzac, Henry James, Melodrama, and the Mode of Excess* (New Haven, CT and London, Yale University Press, 1976), p. 77.

9 Brooks, *The Melodramatic Imagination*, pp. 77–8.

10 This is in no way to question the excellence of Brooks's book nor to deny his own critical self-awareness. For his own account of the methodological problems inherent in his literary-historical undertaking, see *The Melodramatic Imagination*, p. xiii: 'To the extent that literary history addresses itself to the dynamics of a particular genre – its metaphorically biological emergence, flourishing and wane – it can illuminate, especially when it acts as a study of intertextuality, considering the interaction of the texts known as the genre. More often, however, generic history falls victim to its biological metaphor, or to arguments of source and influence, or else to a tracing of thematic constants and their variations.'

11 For one formulation of this argument, see Richard Cronin's article 'Carp and *Caleb Williams*'. Cronin argues that the 'realist novel' is critically presented within Godwin's novel and that it too is revealed to distort the 'reality' it claims to present. I would accept this claim but, in terms of my own argument, what is important is that the novel should be seen as enacting a tension between one genre (chivalric romance) and another (the realist novel) which is in the process of replacing it.

12 See, for example, Marilyn Butler, 'Godwin, Burke and *Caleb Williams*', *Essays in Criticism*, 32 (1982), 237–57.

13 William Hazlitt, originally from the *Examiner* (1 December 1816), reprinted in *A View of the English Stage; or, A Series of Dramatic Criticisms* (1818); quoted from Hazlitt, *The Works of William Hazlitt*, ed. P. P. Howe (London and Toronto, Dent, 1930–34), Vol. V., p. 343.

14 Text from Inchbald's *The British Theatre*, Vol. XXI.

15 See Coleridge, 'Satyrane's letters', Letter II, in *Biographia Literaria or Biographical Sketches of My Life and Opinions*, ed. James Engel and

W. Jackson Bate (London, Routledge and Kegan Paul, 1983), Vol II, p. 190.

16 Inchbald, 'Remarks', p. 2.

17 Cronin, 'Carps and *Caleb Williams*', pp. 44–5.

18 D. A. Millar obseves that there 'is no doubt that the shift in the dominant literary form from the drama to the novel at the end of the seventeenth century had to do with the latter's superior efficacy in producing and providing for privatized subjects', *The Novel and the Police* (Berkeley, CA, University of California Press, 1988), p. 82. My own reading would suggest a continuing tension between the ideological significance of generic choice. See also Deborah Vlock's disagreement with Millar in her *Dickens, Novel Reading, and the Victorian Popular Theatre* (Cambridge, Cambridge University Press, 1998), p. 2. Vlock's work has more direct and sustained relevance to my own study of Dickens in Chapter Four.

19 Jeffrey N. Cox, 'Ideology and genre in the British anti-revolutionary drama of the 1790s', *ELH*, 58 (1991), 579–610, p. 597.

20 Anastasia Nikolopoulou, 'Historical disruptions: the Walter Scott melodramas', in Michael Hays and Anastasia Nikolopoulou (eds), *Melodrama: The Cultural Emergence of a Genre* (New York, St. Martins Press, 1996), p. 137.

21 William Godwin, *Enquiry Concerning Political Justice and Its Influence on Modern Morals and Happiness,* ed. Isaac Kramnick (Harmondsworth, Penguin, 1976), p. 70).

22 Elizabeth Inchbald, letter to William Godwin, quoted in Ford K. Brown, *The Life of William Godwin* (London and Toronto, Dent; New York, Dutton, 1926), p. 86.

23 William Godwin, 'Of History and Romance', ed. Michael Gamer, at http://www.english.upenn.edu/~mgamer/Romantic/godwin.history. html, accessed 3 August 1998. All references are to this edition.

24 Marilyn Gaull, *English Romanticism: The Human Context* (New York and London, W. W. Norton, 1988), p. 93.

CHAPTER TWO

'Another and the same': repetition and representation in adaptations of Scott's *The Lady of the Lake*

WALTER SCOTT'S NARRATIVE POEMS presented the literary world and the book-buying public with an unprecedented phenomenon: no other poems in British history had been so immediately and spectacularly popular. *The Lady of the Lake*, which was first published in an expensive quarto edition in 1810, was even more successful than its two predecessors *The Lay of the Last Minstrel* (1805) and *Marmion* (1808). The quarto edition of *The Lady of the Lake* sold out within days and, within a year, cheaper octavo editions had pushed sales to beyond 20,000 volumes.[1] Such success was accompanied by a large number of adaptations of the poem for the stage, including Thomas Morton's *The Knight of Snowdoun; A Musical Drama, in Three Acts* (1811), Edmund John Eyre's *The Lady of the Lake: A Melo-Dramatic Romance in Three Acts* (1811) and Thomas Dibdin's *The Lady of the Lake. A Drama, in Three Acts* (?1810). In addition to these theatrical adaptations, there was also an anonymous novelisation of Scott's poem as *The Lady of the Lake: A Romance* (1810). These near-contemporary adaptations indicate the obvious popularity of the original poem but, in order to explore more fully their cultural significance, we need to understand the nature of Scott's popularity as a poet and the critical problems that it occasioned. Such problems, as will be seen, are intimately involved both with questions of genre and with emerging distinctions between 'high' and 'low' culture. Before examining the adaptations themselves, therefore, it is necessary to offer an account of the critical controversy caused by his poetry.

THE ENORMOUS SUCCESS of Scott's narrative poetry presented problems for the reviewers for they were being asked to pass judgement upon works that their readers had often already bought and who, in the act of purchase itself, could be seen to be making some form of qualitative assessment. Indeed, for certain critics, Scott's evident popularity was in itself a guarantee of some form of literary value. A review of *Don Roderick* (1811) in the *Quarterly Review* for October 1811, for example, makes the following observations:

> As capricious a nymph as Popularity is often imagined, her favours are not so cheaply purchased as to be the reward of mere sound and tinsel for their own sake; and a wide distinction is to be made in this respect between present popularity and present fame. The last is the decision of the talking and criticising part of society, where favouritism and prejudice may, and must occasionally prevail; the former is the verdict of too numerous a court to be influenced by any unworthy motive, and it is, therefore, though sometimes for a time unjustly refused, yet rarely bestowed erroneously. We often praise a work because we like the author, but we seldom purchase what we are not fond of reading; and therefore, though many a writer has sunk after extravagant applause into utter oblivion, there is, we believe, no instance in works of mere amusement, of the judgment of many editions being in any material degree reversed by posterity.[2]

The reviewer here is in danger of undermining his own critical activity: the work of reviewers, who belong to the 'talking and criticising part of society', is revealed often to be founded upon simple bias and prejudice, whereas the 'judgment of many editions' partakes of a collectively dispassionate and objective assessment which is able to indicate lasting artistic merit. In place of established critical criteria applied by a handful of sensitive and educated critics, the review appears to herald the arrival of a time in which the fluctuations of the literary marketplace are able to bestow the guarantee of poetic immortality.

This is not, of course, the whole story. The review of *Don Roderick* contains within itself its own revealing tensions, not least in its inability to register the distinctly modern nature of the Scott phenomenon. In its evocation of literary precedent ('there is ... no instance ... of the judgment of many editions being ... reversed by posterity'), the review fails to give weight to the fact that no living author had ever before sold 'many editions' in such large numbers in such a short amount of time. This appeal to the past can be read as a rhetorical strategy which provides what is in effect a disturbingly new cultural situation with a reassuring link to previous practices of both reading and writing. Furthermore, in an attempt to deflect the implicit threat to established notions of literary value, the reviewer is careful to limit the effective domain of 'the judgment of many editions' to 'works of mere amusement'. This provides an important swerve from the apparent thrust of the argument up to this point: the literary market place is only able to assess which works are amusing and are likely to continue to be amusing in the years to come; works with a 'higher' purpose might not be popular in the same way but this lack of popularity will not detract from their intrinsic worth.

For many reviewers, of course, the lasting value of any poetic production was dependent upon its 'higher' purpose (however, this was defined) and, as a result, the easy success of Scott's poetry in the marketplace compromised its claim to literary worth: for these reviewers, popularity and high artistic seriousness were antithetical. Thus, for example, a review of *The Lord of the Isles* (1815) in the *Quarterly Review* for July 1815 takes the immediate example of Scott as a starting point for more general observations upon the current state of poetry:

> The works of our modern bards ... are obviously calculated for a much larger description of readers; the characters and sentiments which they contain, the species of interest which they inspire, are, for the most part, level to all capacities; while their faults and deficiencies are such that none but persons of refined and practised taste are in any sensible degree affected by them. Whether this be a sort of merit which indicates great and uncommon talents may perhaps admit a doubt; but at all events it is a very useful one to the public at large.[3]

George Ellis, the reviewer here, is far from celebrating the public utility offered by the 'modern bards': the wider circulation of contemporary poetry has a dissipating effect, he implicitly argues, and it is the role of the critic and reviewer, as representative of those 'persons of refined and practised taste', to remind readers that 'popular' poetry is often not – and perhaps never can be – great poetry. However, if such claims are to be made, there must also be a reinvestigation into those criteria which enable the critic to define and evaluate the 'poetic'. Looking back in 1833 upon critical debates concerning the lasting worth of Scott's poetry, W. B. O. Peabody observed that:

> It has been fashionable enough to say, that the poetry of Scott is not destined to be read hereafter; some infer this from its unusual popularity, as if nothing could be seen aright, except at the distance of a century. Even Sir James Mackintosh, no common judge, believed that it could not last, because none but the most elaborate poetry had yet defied the test of time. This is, after all, only saying, that it does not square with our notions of what poetry ought to be.[4]

Our assessment of what good poetry is, Peabody suggests, is dependent upon 'our notions of what poetry ought to be': the statement is, at one level, disarmingly banal and yet, at another, it strikes at the centre of the difficult problems presented by the Scott phenomenon. If the most prominent and (publicly) successful poet of the age was not writing what could be termed 'real' poetry, what were the implications for a general understanding of the form and function of poetry as an important contemporary genre?

Peabody's own attempt to respond to the question he has implicitly set himself is instructive less in terms of its conclusions than in relation to the strategies he adopts in order to arrive at them. Offering his own views on what constitutes the defining characteristics of Scott's poetry, he notes that 'action is indeed the living soul, which quickens and informs the whole; the heart of his reader beats high as it is born along with the rush and sweep of its movement; and it is vain to say, that there is nothing of poetry in what so excites us, we might as well deny, that there was music in the harp-string of the ancient bard'.[5] At one level, Peabody claims that Scott's poetry is essentially a poetry of 'action': the reader is gripped in the first instance by narrative events and their exciting pace and quasi-physical 'movement'. There is an implied relationship between the 'beat' of the attentive reader's heart and the beat of the poems' rhythmic movement which suggests that the poems' thematic concern with bodily action is matched by a poetic form which appeals primarily to the bodily senses. The reference to the 'ancient bard' can in this context be read as an evocation of the sensual immediacy of Scott's poetic 'music'. However, the bard also serves to link Scott to an established and 'serious' tradition of authoritative poetic utterance. Throughout the passage, there is another level of Peabody's argument which implicitly makes a claim for Scott as more than simply an exciting (and entertaining) poet of 'action' and 'movement'. This alternative claim finds initial expression in the opening paradox: 'Action is ... the living soul.' The paradox lies in the fact that distinctions between external and internal, surface and depth, body and soul are here being confused and confounded. What one could term a similar rhetorical doubleness applies to the allusion to the reader's 'heart': on the one hand, in the sense referred to above, Peabody is alluding to the physical excitement generated by narrative pace; on the other hand, the heart as seat of the emotions makes a fitting companion to poetry which possesses sufficient complexity to possess a 'soul'.

Whilst Peabody wants to make a claim for Scott as a good poet of 'action', therefore, his choice of critical terminology also indicates a suppressed argument for Scott as the kind of poet he was often criticised for not being. Such criticisms are present, for example, in Wordsworth's comments in 1844 as recorded by Lady Richardson: 'as a poet Scott *cannot* live, for he has never in verse written anything addressed to the immortal part of man. In making amusing stories in verse, he will be superseded by some newer versifier; what he writes in the way of natural description is merely rhyming nonsense.'[6] Here Scott is presented as a simple narrative poet whose works fail to address (or contain) anything which can be referred to as the 'soul'. In attacks like these, Scott is often portrayed as a poet of 'surface' rather than 'depth' – as is illustrated by William Hazlitt's account in his essay on Scott from *The Spirit of the Age* (originally published in the *New Monthly Magazine* for April 1824):

> The deep incisions into character are 'skinned and filmed over' – the details are lost or shaped into flimsy and insipid decorum; and the truth of feeling and of circumstance is translated into a tinkling sound, a tinsel *common-place*. ... He has either not the faculty or not the will to impregnate his subject by an effort of pure invention. The execution is much upon a par with the more ephemeral effusions of the press. It is light, agreeable, effeminate, diffuse. ... The definition of his poetry is a pleasing superficiality.[7]

Hazlitt's critical model here – which, despite his ambivalence about the poet, would seem to be close to Wordsworth's – is one which assumes the centrality of emotional or psychological 'depth' in any work which has serious claims to be considered as 'poetry' and it is clear that, according to this model, Scott's poetry is found to be wanting. Like Wordsworth, Hazlitt links the superficial with the ephemeral; only those works which are able to construct a convincing impression of 'depth' are worthy to be differentiated from the mass of mere entertainment that was issuing from the printing presses in increasingly large amounts. Andrea Henderson has more recently attempted to correct the long-standing critical assumption that 'one of the defining features and enduring legacies of Romantic writing is its characterization of the self in terms of psychological depth' and, it is fair to say that Scott, at least in so far as his work is defined by writers such as Wordsworth and Hazlitt, offers an example which challenges such notions of 'Romantic writing'.[8] And yet it is probably also true to say that (to quote Peabody) 'our notions of what poetry ought to be' have largely been defined by this Romantic model of psychological depth.

The subtext of Peabody's defence of Scott's poetry is, therefore, his awareness that the poet fails to fulfil the criteria which were demanded by increasingly hegemonic definitions of the 'poetic'. The next turn in his argument attends more directly to this generic crux:

> The truth is, that it was the development of the same qualities, which were afterwards manifested in his romances with such commanding power, in a form less fitted to reveal them in their full perfection. Fortunate indeed it was, if that can be attributed to fortune, which is an accident of genius only, that he afterwards assumed another form, better calculated for the exhibition of character in all its shifting alternations of light and shade, its infinite varieties of stern feeling, of high resolve, of playful humour, of everything, in short, from the loftiest to the lowest.[9]

The shift here is revealing: having attempted to defend Scott's verse narratives *as poetry*, Peabody suggests that Scott's real power could only be fully revealed when he 'assumed another form', that of the novel (or the romance, as it is termed here).[10] The model which underlies Peabody's formulation is again derived from a Romantic notion of the centrality of the writer-as-informing-genius in that what is presented is a vision of Scott 'assuming' different genres in which to reveal himself. And yet, at the same time, the emphasis has changed from 'action' as the major element of Scott's work to a consideration of the importance of 'character'. The 'depth' which was implicitly lacking in the poetry is seemingly achieved through the complex and wide-ranging depiction of character in the novel. What Scott is implicitly being accused of is an error of generic choice: although Peabody is attempting to champion the poetry there is none the less the suggestion that Scott had chosen the wrong genre and that the novel, as a genre, was better suited for the combination of 'action' and 'character'. Moreover, as a quintessentially bourgeois genre, it was more fitted to the 'much larger description of readers' mentioned by Ellis in his *Quarterly Review* article discussed earlier – and this broader readership was mirrored by the novel's apparent thematic ability to deal with what Peabody calls 'everything ... from the loftiest to the lowest'.

It is clear, therefore, that the unprecedented economic success and cultural prominence of Scott's verse narratives caused difficulties within the critical establishment and that these difficulties ultimately focused upon the definition of poetry as a genre. Retrospectively – and with an awareness of Scott's even greater success as a novelist – critics often presented the problems caused by the poetry in terms of an assumption that the writer had yet to discover the genre that was most suited to his artistic impulses. William Hazlitt, as has been seen, might think that 'the definition of [Scott's] poetry is a pleasing superficiality' but he immediately proceeds to proclaim, 'Not so his NOVELS AND ROMANCES. There we turn a new leaf – another and the same – the same in matter, but in form, in power, how different!'[11] For Hazlitt, 'form' and 'power' are evidently associated with one another and it appears that a generic shift enables Scott to deal with similar (indeed, the 'same') material in a radically different fashion.

Whilst Scott only became a novelist with the anonymous publication of *Waverley* in 1814, contemporary readers of *The Lady of the Lake* could in 1810, the year of the poem's publication, enjoy the experience of what Hazlitt calls 'another and the same' by reading the anonymous novelisation of the poem as *The Lady of the Lake: A Romance ... Founded on the Poem so called by Walter*

Scott. At (nearly) the same time they could also see a range of different adaptations of the poem for the stage (and the popularity of such adaptations continued throughout the century, aided in part by the influence of Rossini's operatic version, *La donna del lago* of 1819). Indeed, whilst the stress of the contemporary critics cited has been upon the 'novelistic' trajectory of Scott's poetry, one could also make a claim for its 'dramatic' qualities. Peabody's emphasis upon action, bodily presence and musicality, for instance, would seem to identify certain 'theatrical' elements which doubtless attracted the many writers of stage adaptations.

However, despite the multiplications of different versions of texts calling themselves 'The Lady of the Lake' (or similar titles), we should not forget that a poem is neither a novel nor a play and that we should take care to heed the important 'otherness' at play within the processes of adaptation. If, as Tzvetan Todorov has maintained, '[g]enres are precisely those relay points by which the work assumes a relation with the world of literature', then a poem, or a novel, or a play will each assume a crucially different relationship with the concept of the literary.[12] In addition, it should not be forgotten that this relationship with the literary is always historically specific in ways which reveal contingent ideological relationships. Thus, for example, whilst George Ellis in the review quoted earlier can implicitly lament the vulgarity of modern, popular poetry, Scott himself, in a letter to Robert Southey in 1819, is capable of exhibiting similar misgivings about the lack of refinement in the contemporary theatre:

> To write for low, ill-informed and conceited actors, whom you must please, for your success is necessarily at their mercy, I cannot away with … Besides, if this objection were out of the way, I do not think the character of the audience in London is such that one could have the least pleasure in pleasing them. One half come to prosecute their debaucheries, so openly that it would degrade a bagnio. Another set snooze off their beef-steaks and port wine; a third are critics of the fourth column of the newspaper; fashion, wit and literature there is not; and on the whole I would rather write verses for my honest friend Punch and his audience.[13]

Scott here voices concern about both the production (the actors) and reception (the audience) of theatrical performance and provocatively claims that he would rather write popular entertainments for children ('verses for my honest friend Punch and his audience') than for an adult audience which fails to display a suitably adult sense of refinement and artistic seriousness. As in the reviews of his own poetry discussed earlier, Scott attempts to define a literary genre both in terms of and against notions of popularity and commercial success: there can be no pleasure (that is, artistic satisfaction and achievement), he argues, in pleasing a vulgar audience despite the fact that success in the theatre would logically seem to be a measure of the value of a dramatic production. The fact that the reviewers had made similar observations about the popularity of his own poetry only underlines the complex ideological relativity at play within the issue of generic choice during this period. At a significant level of debate, writers and critics were engaging with emerging categories of 'high' and 'low' culture which cut across and yet were inflected by a discourse of genre definition. The adaptations of *The Lady of the Lake* – both as play and novel – provide us with an opportunity to observe the processes at work within these reformulations of literary categories.

AN UNSIGNED REVIEW OF *Rokeby* (1813) in the *British Review* for May 1813 compared 'Mr. Walter Scott's muse' with a 'fashionable' young lady who had for some time made herself prominent within society. Noting that her arrival was initially greeted with favour by 'an admiring public', the reviewer proceeds to observe that such admiration was beginning to wane. He regretfully observes that 'something too like disgust is the effect of a monotonous repetition of the same dress, the same airs, and the same fascinations'.[14] As Scott published one enormously successful verse narrative after another, the reviewers began to complain of a weary repetition of the same poetic formula, a repetition which, as the *British Review* goes on to describe, manifested itself both at the macro- and micro-levels of the text:

> We cannot help complaining of his too frequent repetitions of the same images in the same poems. His perpetual recurrence to bowers and towers is perfectly fatiguing; wherever we see the one, we may be sure the other is not far behind. Take away one of his favourite phrases and

a gaping wound would appear in each of his poems. Of all the poets he appears to have the largest interest in the moon; and we cannot help giving him a friendly hint, that if he draws so often upon his funds there, his drafts may come at length to be refused in this planet.[15]

Beyond the criticism of style here there is a tacit awareness of the way in which Scott's poetry is, at an important level, crucially dependent upon elements of repetition, both in terms of subject, plot and narrative and in relation to vocabulary and prosody. The reviewer of *Rokeby* believes that such repetition will harm sales of future poetry and his use of the imagery of economic transaction at the end of the passage quoted above would suggest that Scott is in danger of becoming not only poetically but also financially bankrupt.

However, although sales of Scott's poetry did drop slightly after *The Lady of the Lake*, he remained, by contemporary standards, an extremely popular poet. Perhaps more to the point, therefore, are the observations made by Francis Jeffrey about Scott's proclivity for repetition in his earlier review of *The Lady of the Lake* for the *Edinburgh Review* of August 1810:

> The most popular passages in popular poetry, are in fact, for the most part, very beautiful and striking ... yet they are trite and hackneyed, – they have been repeated until they have lost all grace and propriety, – and, instead of exalting the imagination with the impression of original genius or creative fancy, they only nauseate and offend, by their association of paltry plagiarism and impudent vanity. To the ignorant and careless, the twentieth imitation has all the charm of the original; and that which oppresses the more experienced reader with weariness and disgust, rouses them with all the force and vivacity of novelty.[16]

Unlike the later reviewer of *Rokeby*, Jeffrey effectively distinguishes between two classes of reader who require different kinds of poetry: on the one hand, he posits the existence of an educated and 'experienced reader' who demands that poetry provides evidence of 'original genius and creative fancy'; on the other, he implies the emergence of an 'ignorant and careless' readership which is quite happy to accept – and even to extol the virtues of – 'trite and hackneyed' verse which depends for its apparent artistic success upon the unthinking repetition of prior models. What Jeffrey is developing here, of course, is what has become a recognisable distinction between 'high' and 'low' (or, to use Jeffrey's alternative term, 'popular') culture.

Fundamental to Jeffrey's concept of a 'popular' literature is the element of repetition and this relationship is one which is also to be found in Tzvetan Todorov's more recent analysis of the role of genre in popular culture. Whilst Todorov's work attempts to counter what he perceives to be Romanticism's hostility towards genre classification, he none the less establishes a generic definition of 'high' culture which one could essentially define as Romantic and which is in many ways in keeping with the implicit tenets which lie behind Jeffrey's review. Todorov suggests that the 'major work' or 'masterpiece' is one which 'creates, in a sense, a new genre and at the same time transgresses the previously valid rules of the genre'.[17] Generically, then, the major work partakes of the creativity and originality that Jeffrey identifies as belonging to serious poetry. Against the 'masterpiece', with its transgressive generic tendencies, Todorov places what he terms 'the masterpiece of popular literature':

> As a rule, the literary masterpiece does not enter into any genre save perhaps its own; but the masterpiece of popular literature is precisely the book which best fits its genre. ... If we had properly described the genres of popular literature, there would no longer be an occasion to speak of its masterpieces. They are one and the same thing; the best novel will be the one about which there is nothing to say. This is a generally unnoticed phenomenon, whose consequences affect every esthetic category. We are today in the presence of a discrepancy between two essential manifestations; no longer is there one single esthetic norm in our society, but two; the same measurements do not apply to 'high' art and 'popular' art.[18]

Once again, the key concept here is repetition: the 'popular' masterpiece is one which is capable of repeating the genre to which it belongs and one which has no artistic aspirations to do anything more. Seen from this perspective, Scott's poetry has qualities which would entitle it to be categorized as a 'masterpiece of popular literature' and the difficulties revealed by the many reviewers that have so far been quoted could be ascribed to the fact that, according to Todorov's analysis, Scott's poems provide them with texts about which 'there is nothing to say'. Again, according to Todorov, the reviewers are attempting to judge Scott by the wrong 'esthetic norm', that is, in terms of 'high' rather than 'popular' art. Such a tendency should not be judged too harshly, however: if Todorov, writing in 1966, can write of the bifurcation of literary categories as an 'unnoticed phenomenon' then it is hardly surprising that reviewers in the early nineteenth century should fail to comprehend the nature of a cultural transformation which was only just beginning to make itself felt within society.

However, this is not to claim that the relationship between 'popular' and 'serious' literature was not being debated by contemporary writers and critics. The reviews by Jeffrey and Ellis cited earlier indicate that the issue was perceived to be an important one and Scott himself, in his *Minstrelsy of the Scottish Border* (1803), had contributed to the ongoing debate. In an essay from 1830 entitled 'Remarks on popular poetry' which Scott placed before the original Introduction in later editions of *Minstrelsy of the Scottish Border*, the poet attempts to defend the apparent 'flatness and insipidity' of many border ballads by creating the notion of an original, and much more carefully wrought, poem which has been altered by a series of 'reciters' who have, in repeating the poem, damaged it by limiting it to their own powers of expressive ability. He writes that 'we are authorised to conclude, that in proportion to the care bestowed by the author on any poem, to attain what his age might suppose to be the highest graces of poetry, the greater was the damage which it sustained by the inaccuracy of the reciters, or their desire to humble both the sense and diction of the poem to their powers of recollection, and the comprehension of a vulgar audience'.[19] Whilst Scott here is writing about a different kind of repetition, the underlying principle is similar to that voiced by Francis Jeffrey: the intrinsic artistic worth of an original, imaginative poem is debased by repetition, whether it be repetition by Scott's 'reciters' or Jeffrey's second-rate poets who indulge in 'paltry plagiarism and impudent vanity'. In both cases an index of the level of artistic decline is measured by the appreciative response of a 'vulgar audience'.

In his essay Scott is defending the traditions of poetry which inform his own verse narratives, and the evocation of an artistically worthy original for surviving ballads is, therefore, implicitly a strategy designed to invest those traditions with an aesthetic value which will reflect back on to his own work. Whilst Scott works within the ballad tradition, then, his reading of that tradition places him at the end of a line of inspired original poets rather than their degrading imitators. In his perceptive and suggestive discussion of this issue, Peter Murphy concludes that Scott's poetry 'miraculously reproduces the freedom of orality in a written world ... in spite of always being the same, it is always popular, and in this way imitates the vitality of popular (traditional) forms'.[20] However, the strategy is a dangerous one for, as has been seen, 'repetition' and 'popularity' risk accusations of the very vulgarity that Scott was anxious to avoid. Furthermore, the popularity of Scott's poetry led to yet another kind of repetition in the form of adaptation which, in turn, led to a wider popularity and, given Scott's attitude to theatre audiences quoted earlier, the possibility of yet another form of vulgarity. Scott's account of the apparently degrading processes at play within the transmission of border ballads could be seen to provide an attractive model for the processes of adaptation. Indeed, it is often the case even in the late twentieth century that an adaptation is described as an attempt to limit an original text to (to use Scott's phrase) 'the comprehension of a vulgar audience'. Yet to see adaptation in such dismissive terms is to fail to recognise that in adapting a text from one genre to another, even the most apparently simple adaptation needs to assert what could be termed its own generic genealogy. Moreover, this act of generic self-definition should alert us to the fact that with repetition there must inevitably be significant – and signifying – differences.

Such differences can be observed at all levels of the text. To take a simple initial example, one only has to turn to the changes made to the verse form in Edmund Eyre's 1811 stage adaptation. In his Preface to the play, which was commissioned by Siddons, manager of the Theatre Royal in Edinburgh, Eyre adopts a tone of – perhaps conventional – humility in addressing the poem which has given rise to his adaptation:

> I am very sensible, that Mr. Scott's Poem of 'The Lady of the Lake,' affords materials for a much superior Drama than the one here presented to the public; but as Mr. Siddons, in all his correspondence with me on the subject, urged expedition, I was more attentive to the interest of a Friend, than to the fame of an Author; and the whole piece was arranged, written, and copied, in the short space of ten days.

I can claim little merit beyond that of a compiler. Some few flowrets, indeed (or rather weeds, as the critics may call them, at the foot of Parnassus), are of my own planting; but the praise of poetic ingenuity belongs solely to he Author from whence the scenes, characters, and sentiments have been borrowed. To quote the translated words of Montaigne, which have been appositely applied to similar compositions, I have here only made a nosegay of culled flowers, and have brought little more of my own than the band which ties them.[21]

Eyre here adopts the pose of a simple 'compiler', who has solely brought together passages from Scott's original poetry and presented them in the form of a play. Indeed, the play is very close to Scott's *The Lady of the Lake*, and Eyre's language is throughout heavily indebted to the text he is adapting. However, there is a significant and consistent departure from Scott's verse which carries with it its own generic markings. Early on in Scott's poem, for example, the 'Stranger/Fitz-James' character (later, of course revealed to be King James V) becomes separated from his hunting party and finds himself in a beautiful wilderness. After some senti-mental musing upon the landscape – including the possibility of it being inhabited by a 'sainted hermit' – he turns to more immediate concerns. The relevant section of Scott's poem reads as follows:

> Blithe were it to wander here!
> But now, – beshrew yon nimble deer, –
> Like that same hermit's, thin and spare,
> The copse must give my evening fare;
> Some mossy bank my couch must be,
> Some rustling oak my canopy.
> Yet pass we that; – the war and chase
> Give little choice of resting-place; –
> A summer night, in green wood spent,
> Were but to-morrow's merriment.
> But hosts may in these wilds abound,
> Such as are better missed than found;
> To meet with highland plunderers here
> Were worse than loss of steed or deer, –
> I am alone; – my bugle strain
> May call some straggler of the train;
> Or, fall the worse that may betide,
> Ere now this faulchion has been tried.[22]

In Eyre's adaptation, this becomes:

> Blithe were it then to wander here, but, hold –
> The copse will give me but a lenten fare;
> Some rustling oak must canopy my head,
> Some mossy bank my pillow too must be.
> Well, well, a summer's night thus pass'd in sport,
> Will lengthen out tomorrow's merriment.
> But what if hosts of Highland plunderers
> Should make these wilds their haunts? I am alone,
> No trusty friend beside me, but my sword;
> Well, that, and courage, are my best defence. (I.i, p. 2)

The first thing to notice here is that Eyre's changes are, strictly, unnecessary: Scott has provided a ready-formed soliloquy which could easily be placed in the mouth of a character on the stage. In other adaptations of the time (including that by Dibdin), Scott's verse is adopted without alteration so it is interesting to ask why, given the pressure he was under to complete the play, Eyre chose to give himself additional work. The answer to this question evidently relates to what Eyre saw as the generic demands of the drama as opposed to the verse narrative. In his Preface, Eyre writes of his own 'flowrets' having been interspersed with Scott's original poetry but, from the evidence of the passage quoted above, his contributions seem limited to those which are necessary to alter the verse form rather than add significantly to the content of Fitz-James's speech. Eyre's adaptation appear to indicate that, in his view, rhyming tetrameter lines are unsuitable for the stage (at least for a soliloquy by a central character) and that in order for Scott's poetry to be 'culled' successfully for stage representation, it must be transformed into more traditionally acceptable iambic pentameter blank verse lines.[23] The alterations are not intended to improve or expand upon the original meaning; they are solely a marker of generic transformation, but, as such, they direct the spectator (and the reader) to locate the adaptation within an alternative literary genealogy. In the original poem, Scott asserts his generic genealogy in the three prefatory stanzas to the first canto which take the form of an address to the 'Harp of the North':

O wake once more! how rude so'er the hand
  That ventures o'er thy magic maze to stray;
O wake once more! though scarce my skill command
  Some feeble echoing of thine earlier lay ... (p. 4)

The poet looks back to the kind of poetic tradition that Scott had evoked in *Minstrelsy of the Scottish Border* and, at the same time, relates his work to contemporary artistic interest in the bardic and the primitive. In the theatre, on the other hand, although the dramatist and the audience might share an interest in these contemporary concerns, the immediate generic markers are necessarily different. The adoption of blank verse by Eyre acts as a reminder of pervasive dramatic traditions and, particularly perhaps, the tradition which derives from Shakespeare – a tradition which is called forth more immediately by other aspects of both Eyre's adaptation and that by Thomas Dibdin.

Dibdin, as was noted earlier, is, unlike Eyre, quite content to assimilate Scott's language directly into the fabric of his play, and as a result, when the adaptation is read it often appears as simply an edited and slightly rearranged version of the original poem. However, to read it as such would be to miss the important transformations that take place during the shift from one genre to another. An interesting example of this is provided by the scene in which Fitz-James is entertained by Ellen (the 'Lady of the Lake') in the house of her absent father. Both Eyre and Dibdin dramatise this scene in similar ways but, as Dibdin adopts Scott's language more directly, it is perhaps more instructive to look, in the first instance, at his version. The scene takes place in the 'Hall of the retreat, hung with instruments of war, trophies, skins of animals, &c.', and is worth quoting at length to give an impression of the full effect:

Music. Fitzjames *seems anxious to know of* Margaret *who* Ellen *is; she turns from him; he then enquires of* Ellen, *who refuses to answer, and beckons* Margaret *to retire; they exit.*

FITZ: Sure ne'er did Grecian chisel trace
    A nymph, a naiad, or a grace,
    Of finer form or lovelier face!
    A foot more light, a step more true,
    Ne'er from the heath flower dash'd the dew;
    E'en the slight hare bell rears its head,

Elastic from her airy tread:
What tho' upon her speech there hung
The accents of the mountain tongue, –
Those silver sounds, so soft, so deer [*sic*],
The list'ner holds his breath to hear.
A chieftain's daughter seems the maid;
Her satin snood, her silken plaid,
Her golden brouch such birth betray'd.

Music. Margaret *and* Ellen *enter with a table and refreshments; they invite* Fitzjames *to partake of the repast; he consents; still seems anxious to know who* Ellen *is.*

ELLEN: Weir'd women we! by dale and dawn,
  We dwell afar from tower or town;
  We stem the flood, we ride the blast,
  On wand'ring Knights our spells we cast;
  While viewless Minstrels touch the string,
  'Tis thus our charmed rhymes we sing.

SONG
Allan Bane *(within.)*

Soldier rest! thy warfare o'er,
  Sleep the sleep that knows not breaking;
Dream of battl'd fields no more,
  Days of danger, nights of waking.

Huntsman rest! thy chase is done,
  Sleep! thy hounds are by thee lying;
Sleep! nor dream the setting sun
  Beholds thy gallant steed lie dying.

CHORUS

In our Isle's enchanted Hall,
  Hands unseen thy couch are strewing;
Fairy strains of music fall,
  Every sense in slumbring dewing.

Music. Ellen *and* Margaret *remove the table and repast* – Fitzjames *seems astonished.*

MARG: Stranger, thy bed,
  Within of Mountain heath is spread,
  Its purple flowers shall sweetly shed,
  Their moorland fragrance round thy head;

In paceful [*sic*] sleep thy wand'rings close,
And sink in undisturb'd repose.

Music ... Margaret *offers* Fitzjames *her hand; he follows her.*[24]

The verse here is almost entirely taken directly from Scott, although
the transposition is not a direct one. At a fairly insignificant level,
for example, Dibdin has transposed the opening speech of the
extract from a slightly earlier section of the original narrative
(Canto First, Stanzas XVIII and XIX). Thus, what was ostensibly a
narrational observation of Ellen's beautiful appearance becomes
here a direct commentary by Fitz-James himself. However, such
changes make little material change to the effect of the words as
Scott's narrator is, at this stage, evidently offering the knight's point
of view. In the scene within the hall, Scott creates a sense of mystery
but the nature of this mystery would seem to be of a different order
to that created within the play. The knight having told of the
circumstances which led to him being lost in the forest, Scott's
narrator notes:

> Fain would the Knight in turn require
> The name and state of Ellen's sire;
> [...]
> Each hint the Knight of Snowdoun gave,
> Dame Margaret heard with silence grave;
> Or Ellen, innocently gay,
> Turned all enquiry light away:-
> 'Weird women we! etc. etc. (Canto First, XXX, pp. 36–7)

In Dibdin's version, the two dumbshows, accompanied by music,
create a subtly different effect. The sense of mystery is heightened
to suggest a slightly unnervingly, if none the less enchantingly,
magical ambience: the pervasive music would seem to indicate that
the everyday world has been left behind and that the knight is in the
presence of potentially supernatural forces. Dibdin twice directs the
actor to convey an 'anxious' demeanour and the fact that most of
the communication between him and the women takes place only
through silent physical gesture accentuates the elusive quality they
convey both to Fitz-James and the audience in the theatre. In Scott's
original, the narrational voice helps to diffuse any impression of

potential threat; Ellen is, significantly described as 'innocently gay' and her speech about 'wierd women' is presented as a joke which is part of an attempt to turn 'all enquiry light away'. In Dibdin's adaptation, this speech is presented as far more in keeping with the general atmosphere thus far created: her apparent self-description balances the earlier description of her enchanting beauty by Fitz-James. Scott playfully alludes to a *'belle dame sans merci'* scenario; Dibdin foregrounds the magical possibilities that such a scenario offers. This sense of magic is continued with the song which is sung by the hidden Allan-Bane from 'within'. In the poem, the song is sung not by Allan-Bane but by Ellen herself and thus, whilst Scott notes that the accompanying harp remains 'unseen', the singer of the song is fully present and the song becomes part of the innocent and playful interchange between the hero and heroine. In the theatre, on the other hand, the song emanates from a disembodied voice which follows directly on from Ellen's speech about the 'charmed rhymes' of the wierd women. Moreover, as the song proceeds, the lone voice of Allan-Bane is succeeded by a 'chorus' which serves to emphasise the sense of an 'enchanted Hall' inhabited by a number of supernatural spirits. It is little wonder that the actor playing Fitz-James is directed to appear 'astonished' – the adaptation gives the innocently enchanting atmosphere of the poem a new, more literal, force and, as Fitz-James silently follows Margaret off stage at the end of the scene, he gives every sign of having succumbed to the ambiguously presented charms of the island and its inhabitants.

A handsome, stranded hero, a beautiful, innocent heroine whose father has a position of power on a remote and apparently magical island which is filled with mysterious music: the echoes of *The Tempest* are, it seems, foregrounded when dramatists, aware of their own generic genealogy, attempt to rethink *The Lady of the Lake* in theatrical terms. The same tendency is perhaps even more in evidence in Eyre's adaptation:

CHORUS, *chanted at a Distance, till the Notes gradually become louder.*

> Huntsman, rest! thy chase is done,
> Think not of the rising son;
> For at dawning to assail ye,
> Here no bugles sound reveille.

ALLAN-BANE: The stranger comes! my prophecy's fulfill'd!
   The choristers, obedient to my wish,
   Unseen, salute him with melodious song!

The Door is thrown open, when Fitz-James, *preceded by* Ellen, *enters the Bower. He bows to* Lady Margaret *and the* Minstrel, *and surveys every object with mute surprise, whilst is sung the following.*

          INVISIBLE CHORUS.

In our Isle's enchanted hall,
   Hands unseen thy couch is strewing;
Fairy strains of music fall,
   Ev'ry sense in slumbers dewing.

FITZ-JAMES: 'Tis sure enchantment all! whate'er I hear,
   Whate'er I see, is wrapped in mystery! (I.ii, pp. 5–6)

The song is the same but, again, the effect is very different to that created within Scott's poem. Eyre takes Allan-Bane's prophecy from the original but the way in which it is interpolated within the present scene underlines the effect of disorientating supernaturalism that the dramatist aims to convey. Allan-Bane here becomes a kind of Prospero figure; a quasi-magician who orchestrates the sounds and music of the island to do his bidding. Like his counterpart in Dibdin's version, Fitz-James is struck with 'mute surprise' and, in an addition by Eyre, he only speaks to voice his sense of 'enchantment' and 'mystery'.

However, such magical enchantment works at more than one level. In Eyre's version it is clear that, whilst the display orchestrated by Allan-Bane has the appearance of the supernatural, it is, none the less, a carefully staged performance by a human being which has been arranged as a reception for the knight. The 'invisible' chorus is only so because it cannot be seen by either the Fitz-James or the audience. Similarly, in Dibdin's version, the written text is careful to ascribe the disembodied singing voice to Allan-Bane, whose more corporeal presence will become familiar to the audience as the play continues. The spectators in the theatre, then, are aware that they are watching not 'real' magic but what could be termed 'theatrical' magic, they are responding to the effects of gesture, music and movement that the theatre can uniquely offer. The echoes of plays like *The Tempest* perform a similar function: they act as a reminder of a generic tradition which sets the adaptations within a different genealogy to Scott's poem. If, in that poem, the figure of Allan-Bane functions as a type for the bardic figure that Scott in his prefatory stanzas invokes as the 'Harp of the North' then, in Eyre's play (and implicitly in Dibdin's adaptation too) he performs the role of dramatist who, like Prospero in *The Tempest*, uses his creative ability to provide theatrical spectacle.

As professional dramatists, when Eyre and Dibdin adapt Scott's poem they emphasise elements within it which will most effectively display the defining features of their own genre and thus, at a fundamental level, the adaptations alert their audience to the generic shift enacted by their versions of Scott. In doing this, their acts of 'repetition' necessarily become acts of re-presentation which establish important moments of dissimilarity between themselves and the poetic original. As will be seen, such acts of re-presentation are also implicitly concerned with much broader issues of representation as a whole and, specifically, with the ways in which different genres are crucially predicated upon different modes of representation which can possess quite different cultural resonances and which often in this period relate back to the emerging distinctions between 'high' and 'low' art discussed earlier.

THE 'ADVERTISEMENT' TO Thomas Morton's *The Knight of Snowdoun* (1811) begins with a note of deference which, whilst it is reminiscent of the tone of Edmund Eyre's preface to his own adaptation, is significantly different in terms of its content: 'THIS musical Drama is founded on the Poem of the LADY OF THE LAKE, but as the writer's humble judgment has directed him to select, rather than to copy, he trusts the admirers of the Poem will concede to him the indulgence of making such alterations in the original story, as stage necessity has induced him to adopt.'[25] In fact, it could be argued that Morton goes far beyond what is simply demanded by what he terms 'stage necessity' in that, of the three stage adaptations studied here, his is the one in which deviates the most from both the language and the content of the original upon which it is founded. In addition to giving more space to what are essentially minor (and, in this version, 'comic') characters in Scott's narrative, Morton simplifies the main plot by omitting the character of Malcolm.[26] Malcolm in the poem is Ellen's loved one to whom, despite the attentions of Fitz-James, she remains true until the very last lines in which they are brought together in marriage by the recently undisguised king. Without Malcolm, and with a marriage to the king a historical impossibility, Morton is forced to conclude his adaptation with Ellen's marriage to Roderick Dhu, the fiery highlander whom she consistently rejects in the poem and who is, in fact, killed off by Scott before the end. The result, it has to be said, is not dramatically convincing at the level of character but Morton's representation of Roderick does raise issues which are important for the present argument.

Despite presenting Roderick as a hot-headed advocate of war, Scott is careful to show that he has a strong sense of military honour. This is made particularly evident when the king-in-disguise is attempting to escape from the dangerous highland territory and stumbles across a 'mountaineer' by his fire. The mountaineer elicits from the king that he is an enemy of Roderick Dhu but none the less, despite declaring his own allegiance to the man, he offers to guide the king out of danger. Unknown to the king and, significantly, to the reader, this mountaineer is no other than Roderick Dhu himself. Roderick only reveals himself (and is only revealed to the reader) when, having cleared the dangerous territory, they enter into a further dispute about Roderick and the clansmen and the king declares his readiness to engage in combat with him at the soonest possible moment. The inevitable fight ensues and Roderick is wounded – fatally as it turns out to be. Despite the bloody final outcome, Roderick acquits himself well in this episode and a large part of the effect of Scott's treatment of it is achieved through the limited narrative perspective offered at the beginning. The reader has already encountered Roderick's violent and aggressive temper and so it comes as a surprise to discover that the honourable 'mountaineer' is one and the same man. Scott presents the king's limited viewpoint and his introduction to rough highland honour is reproduced for the reader. In addition, the reader is, by the end of the poem, provided with an additional level of narrative meaning in that s/he is encouraged by this episode to establish parallels between these two (effectively) disguised leaders of men who both reveal a sense of honourable integrity which exists independent of the immediate power bestowed by social rank and station (be it that of king or highland leader).

In adapting *The Lady of the Lake* as *The Knight of Snowdoun*, Morton evidently needed to emphasise those positive aspects of Roderick's character as presented by Scott and yet the narrative strategies adopted by the poet presented logistical difficulties for the dramatist. As a result, Morton was forced by what he terms 'stage necessity' to devise alternative methods for representing Roderick's character. The most obvious immediate problem was that, short of using an elaborate disguise, the audience in the theatre would almost immediately recognise the character of Roderick in the chance meeting with the king. The effect of this would be to destroy the situation of mutual anonymity offered within the poem and would create an alternative form of dramatic irony (enabling the audience to see the situation from Roderick's perspective rather than that of the king). Whilst this might possess an immediate dramatic effect it would lack the complexity of Scott's original.

In response to this problem, Morton attempts a bold move: the first time the audience see Roderick is in the scene where he meets the king and thus, as a unique physical presence on the stage, he has no identity other than that he chooses to reveal during the course of his interaction with the king. In this way the audience's ignorance of who the 'mountaineer' is is maintained. However, as the full effect of Roderick's self-revelation is dependent on the audience's prior knowledge of his character, the earlier scenes are full of quite graphic references to him. To take one example from many, in Act I, Scene ii, the highlander Murdock relays to Ellen Roderick's feelings about her:

> MUR: 'Give me,' (cried my chief) 'but beauteous Ellen's hand, and the Douglas shall not hide in covert, like a hunted quarry – Each mountain clan will make your cause its own – My nuptial song shall be our foeman's dirge – My nuptial torch shall light a thousand villages in flames.'
>
> ELLEN: Dreadful! no more – speak of may father.
>
> MUR: Pointing to me, he frowning said, – 'Dismiss your henchman,' I obeyed. – But now for glorious war.' (I.ii, pp. 19–20)

Such indirect presentations of Roderick provide the audience with an enactment of his character and, at the same time, generate an element of suspense in that they create a desire for the 'real' Roderick to be revealed on stage. And, of course, when this finally does happen they, like the king, mistake him for a simple, if honourable, 'mountaineer'. In this way, Morton's strategy works well as it enables him, at least initially, to portray the less attractive side of Roderick indirectly and to save direct presentation for the moment when Roderick discloses his more worthy characteristics. As a result, his final recuperation in the Morton adaptation is made somewhat more convincing.

However, Morton's tactic functions in other, less plot-specific, ways. The enactment of Roderick's character by other characters within the play has the effect of foregrounding the act of representation itself. Even from the isolated example provided earlier it can be seen that Morton requires his actors to act the part of an (char)actor acting: Murdock's speech goes beyond merely reporting what Roderick said or did, what is indicated is a performance of what he said and did. And such performances are enacted by a range of characters such as the minor character of Norman in Act I, Scene v:

> E'en now Sir Roderick crossed my path – Anguish and rage convulsed his breast – He cried, – 'Ellen, from thee alone will I receive my doom …' (I.v, p. 28)

Like Murdock's earlier rendition, this provides implicit 'stage directions' ('Anguish and rage convulsed his breast – He cried') followed by an impassioned rendition of the actual words spoken. In addition, the actual presence of the woman who is addressed by Roderick's reported/enacted speech gives a heightened sense of immediacy. At such moments, Norman and Murdock are both 'themselves' and not 'themselves'; Roderick is both absent and, paradoxically, present. At a metatextual level, Morton's strategy suggests the paradox which lies at the heart of theatrical representation: the physical presence of actors on the stage embodies the absence of the characters being enacted. However, this insight threatens to undermine the certainty seemingly offered by stage representation for, if all that remains is a 'performance' which cannot guarantee any underlying 'truth', how can any final, fixed judgements about 'character' be made?

These issues are, of course, intimately connected with the thematic concerns of *The Lady of the Lake* and *The Knight of Snowdoun* (and, indeed, the other adaptations) in that both texts have at their centre a king who, for most of the narrative, performs the role of a simple knight and whose character is judged, by both readers and spectators, on the nature of that performance. As a play, however, the adaptation more obviously foregrounds such problems and asks its audience to consider the possibility that the only 'truth' which can ultimately be known is that which can be conveyed through 'performance'. The generic implications of this possibility will be considered in the next section but, before that, it is instructive to give a further twist to the present discussion of Roderick's representation in *The Knight of Snowdoun*. It was noted earlier how Morton has attempted to recreate in dramatic terms the narrative techniques deployed by Scott in his poem. As a result the spectator in the theatre will, despite having a knowledge of Roderick's character, not recognize him when he is first revealed in the scene where he meets the king in disguise. However, this is to assume that the spectators have not read Scott's poem. If they have, and this would be quite likely given its enormous popularity, then what they 'see' when the curtain rises on the unidentified 'warrior' of Act II, Scene i is an actor playing Roderick (a character in a poem they have read) playing an unidentified warrior. In this instance, the act of repetition brought about by adaptation heightens an awareness of both re-presentation and representation.

IN THE FINAL CANTO OF Scott's *The Lady of the Lake*, Allan-Bane the minstrel visits the dying Roderick, who has been imprisoned by the king's forces. Roderick briefly asks him to sing an account of the battle that had recently taken place between the highlanders and the forces loyal to the king. This Allan-Bane does at length but, suddenly, he comes to an abrupt halt:

> But here the lay made sudden stand,
> The harp escaped the Minstrel's hand! –
> Oft had he stolen a glance, to spy
> How Roderick brooked his minstrelsy:
> At first, the Chieftan, to the chime,

With lifted hand, kept feeble time;
That motion ceased, – yet feeling strong
Varied his look as changed the song;
At length, no more his deafened ear
The minstrel melody can hear;
His face grows sharp, – his hands are clenched,
As if some pangs his heart-strings wrenched;
Set are his teeth, his fading eye
Is sternly fixed on vacancy; –
Thus, motionless, and moanless, drew
His parting breath, stout Roderick Dhu! –
Old Allan-bane looked on aghast,
While grim and still his spirit passed;
But when he saw that life was fled,
He poured his wailing o'er the dead. (Canto Sixth, XXI, pp. 275–6)

This 'wailing' takes the form of a spontaneous poetic outpouring which is differentiated from the preceding text by the designation 'Lament' in Gothic typeface. The significant element of this scene for the present discussion is its degree of generic self-consciousness. It has already been noticed in passing that Allan-Bane plays the role of Scott's surrogate within the poem in that he is a type for the bardic 'Harp of the North' that Scott calls upon in the opening stanzas. Within the present scene, Scott foregrounds such bardic poetry as a mode of representation. The battle which the minstrel describes for Roderick has already taken place earlier in the poem's 'action' but the temporal delay accentuates the reader's awareness that what is being conveyed is a poetic representation of a 'real' event and that such representations are designed for a specific audience and in order to create specific effects. The emotional content of the scene is also explicitly mediated through the production and reception of poetry. Thus, an understanding of the fluctuating passions felt by Roderick in his final moments is dependent upon readers having experienced for themselves the modulations of Allan-Bane's account of the battle which precedes the relatively short account of the death itself. Similarly, the grief caused by Roderick's death finds immediate expression in and through the minstrel's poetic 'lament'. The scene thus indicates the role of poetry as a means of conveying historical 'fact' in an emotionally heightened form and also as a mode for creating communities of shared emotional allegiance. In a way which confirms the opinions of many of the reviewers quoted earlier, the poetry does not attempt to suggest the 'depth' of such emotions: Roderick's response to the minstrel's lay is measured in relation to the movement of his hand or the way in which he 'varied his look as changed the song', and the physicality of such responses is reminiscent of W. B. O. Peabody's description of how 'the heart of the reader [of Scott's poetry] beats high as it is born along with the rush and seep of its movement'.

At a metatextual level, therefore, one can see Scott's account of Roderick's death as offering a poetic programme for the form and function of his own poetic practice. At the same time, the emphasis upon physical gesture and movement could also be seen as providing a point of entry for the dramatist who was attempting to adapt the poem for the stage. In light of this, it is interesting to think about the same scene as it is represented by Edmund Eyre. As in Scott's original, Eyre has Allan-Bane sing an account of the battle to the dying Roderick, but the song is preceded by the following stage direction:

SONG OF THE BATTLE – ALLAN-BANE
accompanied on the Harp

(In the following Song, instead of the usual Symphonies between each Verse, the Music is to play Notes expressive of that Passion, which every Stanza has excited in the mind of Roderick) (I.iv, p. 46)

After Allan-Bane's song, there are further stage directions which inform the actor playing Roderick how the character's death is to be performed:

During the last four lines, Roderick's features and gestures become violently agitated – at the last, he starts from the Couch, tears the Bandages from his Wounds, clenches his hands, and sternly fixing his eyes upon vacancy, falls back, and expires without a groan – Music to the whole of the Action. (I.iv, p. 46)

Although in Scott's poem Allan-Bane's song and Roderick's death take place simultaneously, they are presented consecutively and, as has been suggested, the reader's experience of the song is a prerequisite for the emotional response required by the death scene which follows it. In the theatre 'stage necessity' effectively requires the simultaneous presentation of song and death (if Scott's poem is to be adapted 'faithfully' that is) and yet such simultaneity, as it is offered by Eyre, presents a very different representation of emotion. In the poem, poetry itself is the medium through which emotion is expressed (a self-evident statement but one which Scott foregrounds in terms of his own poetic programme); in the theatre, the song might be the occasion for Roderick's emotion but it is not the vehicle through which it is conveyed. His emotional response is represented, not through the modulations of the song itself, but through separate music which is designed to be 'expressive of that Passion, which every Stanza has excited' in his mind. The second stage direction indicates that, in addition to the use of music, emotion is represented through accompanying movement and gesture. Interestingly, Eyre adopts many of the physical elements of Scott's own description – such as the clenched hands or the fixing of his eyes 'upon vacancy'. At the same time, whilst Eyre's Roderick, like Scott's, 'expires without a groan', his final actions are far more expressive of inner turmoil: 'he starts from the Couch, tears his Bandages from his Wounds ...' As a result of such changes, in the theatre the song takes second place to the enactment of emotion through dumbshow and accompanying expressive movement. If Scott, in the eyes of the reviewers, had failed to create 'true' poetry because of his 'superficiality' and lack of 'depth', on the stage such use of action and movement becomes a crucial form of representation. 'Character' on stage is not an issue of inner 'truth' or revealed 'depth' but, rather, one of a performance which is dependent upon movement and gesture and the sensual immediacy of expressive music.

Eyre's adaptation reveals significant differences in modes of representation which, at this moment in literary history, are almost inevitably present when a work is adapted from one genre to another. The fact that the theatre is dependent upon what could be termed more 'superficial' modes of representation goes some way to account for its decline in status as a 'serious' art form at a time when the construction of inner truth and depth appeared increasingly to bestow artistic worth. In relation to this it is instructive to compare and contrast the same scene of Roderick's death as it is

presented in the anonymous novelisation of *The Lady of the Lake*
dating from 1810. In this 'Romance', the old minstrel similarly
visits the dying Roderick in prison and asks him how he 'was lost':

> 'I'll tell thee then,' cried the feeble Roderick, faintly, who, after many
> struggles, raised his weak body, while his eyes were inflamed with the
> fever which had seized him – his swarthy face was chequered with pale
> and ghastly streaks, while the voice which lately boasted of broad and
> manly tones now dwindled into faint and childish accents.
>
> 'Alas! old man, I who have withstood numbers in the field have been
> conquered in a single combat. A stranger, who twice presumed to enter
> our ground without permission, and who therefore was judged to be a
> spy, has deprived me of my liberty, and, I may say too, of my life.'[27]

Whilst some of the details here derive from Scott's poem (compare
Scott's 'ghastly, pale, and livid streaks / Chequered his swarthy
brow and cheeks' at Canto Sixth, XIV, p. 262), the most obvious
initial reaction to this adaptation is the way in which the novelist
has felt the need to expand upon the original. In part this is perhaps
dictated by market expectations about the length of a novel, but,
none the less, the nature of the additions are interesting. The novel
provides Roderick with a more distinctive and sustained voice in
his final scene, allowing him more space to convey his thoughts and
feelings directly through his own words. In addition to this, the
expanded descriptions, whilst predominately consisting of an
account of external features, are used to suggest the psychological
changes that have taken place within Roderick as a result of his
defeat. Thus the fact that his voice has been transformed from
'broad and manly tones' to 'faint and childish accents' indicates not
simply the diminishment of physical power but a mental change
which indicates both an awareness of physical weakness and the
fact that, in the approach to death, his warlike temperament has
been tempered by something approaching a newly rediscovered
childlike innocence. The Roderick of the novel also asks Allan-Bane
to give an account of the battle but, this time, it is he who calls for
it to stop:

> 'Hold, hold, old man!' replied the chief, in feeble accents, while he held
> out his trembling hand, 'the pangs of death are on me; yes, yes, I feel
> them wrenching my very heart-strings.'

His face now became sharp, and his hands were clenched together.
'Yes, yes,' he resumed, 'I have had my death-wound; that stranger –
didst ever learn his name?'
'The Knight of Snowdoun he called himself.'
'Ha! the Knight of Snowdoun, I guess; yes, yes, I guess who was my foe,
the Knight of Snowdoun is —— —— Oh, my head swims, my eyes grow
dim, I – I – I – can speak no more.'

His teeth now chattered, his eyes began to close, he grasped for
breath, then motionless sunk down. (pp. 105–6)

Again, certain elements are derived almost directly from Scott and
yet, again, Roderick is given far more prominence as a thinking and
feeling protagonist. Whilst Scott writes of Roderick behaving '*As if*
some pang his heart-strings wrenched' (emphasis mine), the novelist allows Roderick to express this as a fact and, in general, there
appears to be a need for the novel to present the highlander as far
more self-conscious and, in its limited way, more psychologically
complex. The major addition to the scene seems to be designed to
further this end. In Scott's poem Roderick dies not knowing who
his assailant was, here he possesses an unexplained and rather
mysterious insight which (in theory) indicates a knowledge which is
superior to that of both the reader and the other characters at this
point in the narrative. There are 'depths' to Roderick's understanding which, thanks to the rather ambiguous dashes in the text, he
takes with him to the grave. In a rather clumsy way, what one
might term the mystery of plot (who is the knight of Snowdoun?)
becomes, in addition, a marker of the mysterious depths of a
particular character's mind.

Scott's detractors and critics saw his poetry as failing the
demands of 'high' art because it displayed qualities which could be
seen as superficial and repetitious. Such qualities did not, however,
reduce the enormous popularity of the poems themselves and, it
could be claimed that, since the Romantic period, these very qualities have become defining features of what has come to be called
'popular' culture. One result of Scott's popularity was the large
number of adaptations of his work, some of which have been
focused upon in the present discussion. Such adaptations represent
another form of 'repetition' which is both related to and distinct
from the repetitive element within 'popular' art. It is distinct in so
far as the act of repetition in another genre necessarily creates

crucial differences between the original poem and the adaptation. These differences are intimately connected with issues of genre choice. The stage adaptations discussed here develop what were seen disparagingly as the 'superficial' elements within Scott's poetry in order to further a theatrical practice which based its mode of representation upon gesture, movement and expressive music. On the other hand, in the novelisation of *The Lady of the Lake* one can detect a reversal of this tendency: the novel, as genre, appears to redirect its reader's attention towards issues of 'character' and psychological 'depth'. Many critics, as has been noted, retrospectively saw Scott's failure as a poet in terms of a failure of generic choice: as the novelist he later became he fulfilled their criteria for what constituted a successful 'serious' writer. However, rather than seeing this simply as the idiosyncratic choice of 'genius' (as did W. B. O. Peabody), one might begin to construct a generic history in which, at a specific moment in time, certain generic choices entailed certain modes of representing human beings which were, in turn, invested with different cultural values. It is important to keep this in mind as we move to a consideration of Scott's 'historical' novels and the stage adaptations to which they gave rise.

Notes

1 Here and elsewhere, I am much indebted to Peter Murphy's chapter on Scott in his *Poetry as an Occupation and an Art in Britain 1760–1830* (Cambridge, Cambridge University Press, 1993).

2 Review of *The Vision of Don Roderick; a Poem*, *Quarterly Review*, VI (October 1811) 224–5.

3 Review of *The Lord of the Isles*, *Quarterly Review*, XIII (July 1815) by George Ellis, quoted in John O. Hayden (ed.), *Scott: The Critical Heritage* (London, Routledge, 1970), p. 90.

4 W. B. O. Peabody, Unsigned review of Allan Cunningham's *Some Account of the Life and Works of Sir Walter Scott*, *North American Review*, XXXVI (April 1833), quoted in Hayden (ed.), *Scott*, p. 336.

5 Peabody, in Hayden (ed.), *Scott*, p. 337.

6 Wordsworth, recorded by Lady Richardson, 12 July 1844, quoted in Hayden (ed.), *Scott*, p. 381

7 William Hazlitt, 'Scott', No. IV in a series entitled 'The sprits of the age', in the *New Monthly Magazine*, X (April 1824), quoted in Hayden (ed.), *Scott*, pp. 280–2.

8 Andrea K. Henderson, *Romantic Identities: Varieties of Subjectivity, 1774–1830*, (Cambridge, Cambridge University Press, 1996), p. 1.

9 Peabody, in Hayden (ed.) *Scott*, p. 337.

10 The term 'romance' provides Scott's movement from poetry to novel with an apparent sense of continuity, suggesting a link between the verse romance on the one hand and the novel-as-romance on the other. The terms 'novel' and 'romance' (and the related term 'history') were, of course the subject of much critical debate during the period.

11 Hazlitt, 'Scott', in Hayden (ed.) *Scott*, p. 282.

12 Tzvetan Todorov, *The Fantastic: A Structural Approach to Literary Genre*, trans. Richard Howard (Cleveland, OH, Case Western Reserve Press, 1973), p. 8.

13 Scott, letter to Southey, April 1819, quoted in Michael R. Booth, Richard Southern, Frederick and Lise-Lore Marker and Robertson Davies, *The Revels History of Drama in English: Volume VI, 1750–1880* (London, Methuen, 1975), p. 194.

14 Review of *Rokeby*, *British Review*, IV (May 1813), in Hayden (ed.), *Scott*, p. 62.

15 Review of *Rokeby*, in Hayden (ed.), *Scott*, p. 66.

16 Francis, Jeffrey, review of *The Lady of the Lake*, *Edinburgh Review*, XVI (August 1810), quoted in Murphy, *Poetry as an Occupation and an Art*, p. 157.

17 Tzvetan Todorov, 'The typology of detective fiction', from *The Poetics of Prose*, trans. Richard Howard (Cornell University Press, 1977) quoted in David Lodge, *Modern Critical Theory: A Reader* (London, Longman, 1988), p. 158.

18 Todorov, 'The typology of detective fiction', quoted in Lodge, *Modern Critical Theory*, p. 159.

19 Scott, 'Remarks on popular poetry', quoted in Murphy, *Poetry as an Occupation and an Art*, pp. 148–9.

20 Murphy, *Poetry as an Occupation and an Art*, p. 153.

21 *The Lady of the Lake: A Melo-Dramatic Romance, in Three Acts; Taken from the Popular Poem of that Title, And now Performing with undiminished applause, at the Theatre Royal, Edinburgh*, by Edmund John Eyre, formerly of Pembroke College, Cambridge; and now of Drury-Lane and Hay-Market Company of Comedians. (London, W. H. Wyatt, 1811), n.p.

22 Walter Scott, *The Lady of the Lake. A Poem* (10th edn, Edinburgh, Longman, Hurst Rees, Orme and Brown, 1814), Canto First, Stanza XVI, pp. 20–1.

23 In a letter to an actress who was to appear in what was, presumably, Dibdin's adaptation, Scott discussed the effect of Eyre's change in

metre: 'The words of the poem were retained but as they were thrown into the arrangement of blank verse the dialogue had to those acquainted with the poem the appearance of an old friend with a new face. You always missed the expected and perhaps remembered rhyme which had a bald effect.' Letter to Miss Smith, Edinburgh, 12 March 1811, in Scott, *The Letters of Sir Walter Scott*, ed. H. J. C. Grierson (London, Constable, 1933), Vol. II, p. 463.

24 *The Lady of the Lake. A Drama, in Three Acts; Founded on the Popular Poem written by W. Scott, Esq. Arranged as it is now performed, at the Theatre-Royal, Dublin. Revised from the Prompt Book, by Permission of the Manager* (Dublin, J. Charles, n.d.). The British Library ascribes this to Dibdin and dates it ?1810), pp. 7–8.

25 *The Knight of Snowdoun; A Musical Drama, in Three Acts, As it is performed at the Theatre Royal, Covent Garden.* By Thomas Morton (London, Sharpe and Hailes, 1811), n.p.

26 In the letter to Miss Smith quoted earlier, Scott also discusses this aspect of the Morton adaptation: 'I am told Roderick recovers and marries Ellen there being no Malcolm Graeme in the case. You must know this Malcolm Graeme was a great plague to me from the beginning – you ladies can hardly comprehend how very stupid lovers are to every body but mistresses – I gave him that dip in the Lake by way of making him do something but wet or dry I could make nothing of him. His insignificance is the greatest defect among many others in the poem. But the canvas was not broad enough to include him considering I had to groupe the King, Richard and Douglas.' (Scott, *Letters*, Vol. II, p. 464).

27 *The Lady of the Lake: A Romance*, in Two Volumes. Founded on the Poem so called by Walter Scott, Esq. (London, Thomas Tegg, 1810), Vol. II, pp. 85–6.

CHAPTER THREE

Adapting the national myth:
stage versions of Scott's *Ivanhoe*

WALTER SCOTT'S *Ivanhoe* proved to be one of his most popular novels in terms of the number of successfully staged adaptations which appeared in the century following its original publication in late December 1819. In his catalogue of Scott dramatisations, Richard Ford lists thirty-seven stage plays, musicals and burlesques which were based on the novel in the period between 1820 and 1913;[1] in his earlier seminal study of the plays, Henry Adelbert White notes that this particular novel 'aroused a greater number and a wider range of dramatic adaptations than any other Scott production'.[2] However, it is not simply the number and range of productions which is remarkable, but also the speed with which playwrights and playhouses were able to offer their audiences a stage version of the latest volumes from the 'Great Unknown' (as Scott still, officially, was). Little over a month after the novel's publication, Thomas Dibdin's play, *Ivanhoe; or, The Jew's Daughter*, appeared, on 20 January 1820, at the Surrey Theatre to be followed, on 24 January, by another adaptation, possibly W. T. Moncrieff's *Ivanhoe; or, The Jew of York*, at the Coburg Theatre. In the 'Advertisement' to the published text of his play, Dibdin comments upon the successful teamwork which lay behind it:

> THIS opportunity is eagerly seized of again publicly thanking the inde-
> fatigable zeal, union, and ability, evinced by every member of the Surrey
> Theatre, in all its departments, towards the production of Ivanhoe,
> which was more perfectly accomplished through such determined and
> spirited assistance, and in a shorter period than perhaps there is any
> precedent for.[3]

Once again, one can see how Scott's work has repercussions which are seen by contemporaries as unprecedented. Dibdin highlights the enormous artistic and material investment that went into such adaptations, investments which theatre companies no doubt believed would be fully returned with significant interest. The speed with which *Ivanhoe* reached the stage, therefore, attests both to the rapidity of the novel's circulation and to the public's immediate acceptance of it as a popular work that they would readily agree to experience again in another genre. And it should not be thought that such reworkings of the novels were restricted to the (perhaps) less serious 'illegitimate' theatres: on 2 March 1820 two further adaptations of *Ivanhoe* appeared, one by Samuel Beazley (*Ivanhoe; or, The Knight Templar*) at Covent Garden, and the other by George Soane (*The Hebrew*) at Drury Lane. In the early decades of the nineteenth century at least, Scott's work was 'legitimate' material for all sections of the British theatrical world.

Scott's own attitude to what he termed on one occasion his 'theatrical grandchildren' was far from being clear-cut.[4] He evidently enjoyed the contemporary theatre and he is on record as having attended a number of stage versions of his novels and poems.[5] Of particular interest in light of the present discussion is the French operatic version of *Ivanhoe* (by E. Deschamps and G. G. de Wailly with a selection of music by Rossini) which Scott saw when he was in Paris in 1826 and about which he writes quite favourably in his Journal:

> In the evening at the Odeon where we saw *Ivanhoe*. It was superbly got up, the norman soldiers wearing pointed helmets and what resembled much hauberks of mail which looked very well. The number of attendants and the skill with which they are moved and grouped upon the stage is well worthy of notice. It was an opera and of course the story greatly mangled and the dialogue in great part nonsense. Yet it was strange to hear anything like the words which I (then in an agony of pain with spasms in my stomach) dictated to William Laidlaw at Abbotsford now recited in a foreign tongue and for the amusement of a strange people.[6]

What Scott obviously enjoyed in the performance that he saw was the element of spectacle, the distinctly 'theatrical' aspects of the opera such as costume, movement and the grouping of figures upon the stage for visual effect. However, at the same time as he responded positively to these aspects, he also registers misgivings about what one might term the more 'literary' elements of the production: the 'story' is 'mangled' and the 'dialogue' is judged to be 'in great part nonsense'. For Scott this appears as almost an inevitability, the necessary sacrifices a playwright (or librettist) will have to make in order to adapt the novel for the stage. None the less, the effect of this performance in Paris also possesses a potentially disturbing subtext: Scott has an uncanny sense of meeting an earlier self which is both familiar and strange; the opera presents him with a mirror in which he both recognises and fails to recognise his own creative labour. *Ivanhoe* had, it seemed, become 'foreign', and not simply at the level suggested by a literal translation from one language to another.

Scott's unease is not only caused by the strangeness of his 'own' words, it is also a result of those words being performed 'for the amusement of a strange people'. Another, slightly earlier, journal entry from Scott provides further insight into this aspect of his response. In an entry dated 23 November 1825, Scott observes:

> Talking of Abbotsford it begins to be haunted by too much company of every kind. But especially foreigners. I do not like them. I hate fine coats and breast pins upon dirty shirts. I detest the impudence that pays a stranger compliments and harangues about his works in the Author's house, which is usually ill breeding. Moreover they are seldom long of making it evident that they know nothing about what they are talking of excepting having seen the *Lady of the Lake* at the Opera.[7]

Scott begins here by complaining about certain occurrences which are, in effect, the consequences of his enormous popularity as a writer. His home is invaded by literary tourists and, more to the point, they have the audacity to claim opinions about the works which they have purchased. Scott evidently feels imposed upon, not only his land but his work have been violated by a public who believe they have a share in the literary productions which are now part of the public domain. The rhetorical strategy of Scott's journal entry is to conflate issues of class ('ill breeding') and race. The immediate object of hatred is the 'foreigner', but it is clear that there is a wider fear of an ill-bred and ill-educated audience at home and this disturbing undercurrent suggests that the 'foreigner' can belong to one's own country. Significantly for the present discussion, Scott conveys this sense of similarity and difference through the introduction of an adaptation ('they know nothing about what they are talking of excepting having seen the *Lady of the Lake* at the Opera'). Knowing an author's works only through their stage adaptations becomes an index of one's social inferiority and one's ill-breeding; such people have no right to claim affinity with the world to which the author belongs. Such people do not speak the same language.

Although Scott often encouraged and supported his friend Daniel Terry's attempts to earn money through adaptations of the novels, his attitude to the adaptations themselves is generally in keeping with the subtextual implications of these two journal entries. In a letter to Terry dated 18 May 1818, Scott discusses how he will send the playwright proofs of his next novel in order to provide him with a head start in the race to the stage:

> You shall have the new Tales as soon as the first story is completely in proof & you must beg to secure the ear of your manager before other competitors come to dramatize the book. It is a singular & I think bad way of amusing the public in point of taste but that is no good reason why you should not make the most of the many headed brute & show before him such forage as his sort for the time is disposed to delight in.[8]

Scott colludes in the process of adaptation here, and demonstrates a clear sense of the workings of the theatrical market, and yet he has no delusions about what he perceives to be the inferior artistic status of the adaptation as a theatrical form. The popularity of adaptations is seen as a sign of a decline in aesthetic 'taste', a product demanded by a brutish and undiscriminating public and only worth creating in order to make money. The irony here, of course, is that very similar criticisms were being directed at Scott and his novels. In the 'Introductory Epistle' to *The Fortunes of Nigel* (1822), Scott, in the persona of the 'Author', feels the need to defend himself against charges of financial greed and lack of artistic quality. In defence against the second charge, he writes that it 'is some consolation to reflect, that the best authors in all countries have been the most voluminous; and it has often happened, that those who have been best received in their own time, have also continued to be acceptable to posterity. I do not think so ill of the present generation, as to suppose that its present favour necessarily infers [sic] future condemnation.'[9] This view of the 'present generation' sits uneasily alongside the 'many headed brute' that Scott writes of in his letter to Terry. In order to justify his own popularity in the face of what he sees as a depraved popular taste for extravagant and superficial theatrical productions, Scott has to adopt a double vision in which certain aspects of popularity bestow value whereas others are a sign of its opposite. Such manoeuverings lead to an unstable sense of who exactly constitutes an author's 'audience' and, perhaps even more worrying for an author, how that audience reads the works themselves. Scott's disorientation in Paris when confronted with his own words 'recited in a foreign tongue and for the amusement of a strange people' is perhaps part of a larger sense of (British) cultural dislocation in the early decades of the nineteenth century.

Chris R. Vanden Bossche reminds us that *Ivanhoe* 'dramatizes culture as a semiotic system that constitutes social relations. The novel's protagonists are not just Cedric, Wilfred, Bois-Guilbert, and Isaac of York, but the languages they speak: Saxon, the lingua franca, Norman, and Hebrew.'[10] Scott's novel, in its broadest outlines, attempts to provide contemporary England with a cultural (and linguistic) genealogy through which his contemporaries can perceive the unified nation which has developed through a successful synthesis of initially competing discourses. Such synthesis, however, would appear to be at odds with the fear of the 'foreigner within' that the present discussion has located within Scott's own writing. As has been seen, the popularity of his work, and the repercussions of such popularity, raise questions about the extent to which the nation, as represented by the possibility of a shared aesthetic 'taste', was indeed a unified entity. The existence of so many adaptations of the novels helps to focus some of these questions in that, as Scott perhaps recognised in Paris, adaptations translate the 'language' of the novel into their semiotic system which produces an uncanny sense of similarity and difference, of the familiar and the foreign.

The present chapter will look at some of the ways in which Scott's novels were considered to be 'theatrical' by contemporary critics and thus could be said to provide suitable material for adaptation. However, as will be seen, it is misleading to overemphasise the affinities between the novels' formal qualities and those of the theatre: the work of Georg Lukacs on the crucial formal and ideological differences between the genres of novel and drama therefore provides a helpful starting point for a consideration of the form and function of the Scott adaptations. Having established a contextual and methodological framework, the chapter will continue with an examination of two specific adaptations – one from the 'illegitimate' theatre, by Thomas Dibdin, and one, by George Soane, from the 'legitimate' theatre. Dibdin's play offers a reasonably straightforward adaptation which none the less implicitly conveys different ideological nuances through the processes at work when Scott's narrative is generically transformed. George Soane's *The Hebrew*, on the other hand, provides a more ambitious reworking of *Ivanhoe* in which questions of race and national identity are dealt with in a more explicit and provocative fashion.

THE PROXIMITY OF THEIR first reading of the novel and the performance of Thomas Dibdin's *Ivanhoe; or, The Jew's Daughter* at the Surrey Theatre in January 1820 would have enabled an audience to make quite rigorous and detailed comparison of the two works. This is something of which Dibdin is acutely aware in the opening address, spoken by an actress who, she claims, has been requested by the playwright to

> Ask your friends, the audience, to reflect
> On what we've undertaken – don't neglect
> To urge, 'twas very few short days ago
> Since first in print, appeared Sir Ivanhoe;
> How much we've had to do, to think and write,
> Compose, rehearse, paint, sew, embroider, and what not
>   to bring him here to-night –
> Tell 'em, too, we are fearfully aware
> That every Reader, above all the Fair,
> Will look for this, or that scene, which our space
> Of time, and limit, may not yield a place
> And each will think the subject we neglect,
> Unless they see what, they most affect –

Now 'Gentlemen and Ladies,' tho 'tis true
I'm angry with the bard, I must tell you
If three thick volumes in three Acts you ask,
It may be, probably, no easy task
Your wishes, to 'fulfil – and that no man
Can offer better, than the best he can ... (pp. vii–viii)

Dibdin comments not simply upon the material difficulties of producing the adaptation (the composing, rehearsing, painting, sewing and embroidering) but also upon the practical difficulties posed for the writer himself. The 'space' of the stage is, he notes, a limited one, not simply in terms of physical size but also in terms of the time which can be allotted to for each performance. Such observations on the limitations of the stage are not, of course, entirely original: one might, for example, wish to relate Dibdin's remarks here with the famous opening speech of Shakespeare's *Henry V* in which the Chorus laments the restrictions of the 'wooden O' of the Shakespearean theatre. However, a crucial difference between the two passages is that whereas Shakespeare is discussing the inability of stage representation to do full justice to 'real' life, Dibdin is explicitly making a comparative judgement upon the imaginative limits of two distinct genres. It is quite clear, he implies, that the imaginative possibilities of 'three thick volumes' cannot be accommodated within the confines of 'three Acts'. However, despite this element of generic opposition, Dibdin implicitly reads Scott's novel in terms of what one might call its theatrical elements. The 'Reader' (and one must remember that this refers not to the reader of Dibdin's published play but to the reader of Scott's *Ivanhoe*) is expected to be primarily affected by, not character or plot, but 'this, or that scene'. The implication is that Scott's novels are read, at least in part, as a series of discrete set-pieces which can be transformed into similar 'scenes' within the theatre. This provides a very simple model for the process of adaptation and one which suggests an unproblematic formal relationship between the genres of novel and drama. Such an approach is criticised by W. T. Moncrieff in the Preface to his slightly later adaptation of *Ivanhoe*, when he observes that many playwrights have 'obtained the reputation of excellent Dramatists, on no better ground than paste, shears, and a Scotch novel'.[11] It would appear from Dibdin's opening address that he is in danger of being included within the group of dramatists who form the target of Moncrieff's attack.

Having said this, it has to be acknowledged that contemporary critics of Scott's novels did discuss them in dramatic terms. In particular, they often lamented what they took to be certain excessively theatrical elements within the fiction which would perhaps make them suitable for the kind of treatment that Moncrieff attacks. J. L. Adolphus, for example, in his book-length comparison of Scott's novels and poems which was published anonymously in 1822, identifies within all of Scott's work what he refers to as 'an over-ambitious seeking after what are technically called coupsde-theatre'. These, he claims, are 'not properly dramatic, but melodramatic' and he proceeds to give an example from *Ivanhoe* to support his case:

> In *Ivanhoe*, when the castle of Front-de-boeuf is wrapped in flames, and its besiegers stand waiting for its downfall, behold! the Saxon Ulrica, by whose hand the conflagration was kindled, appears on the turret, 'in the guise of one of the ancient furies, yelling forth a war-song,' her hair disheveled, and insanity in her eyes. Brandishing her distaff, she stands ... among the crashing towers, till, having finished several stanzas of her barbarous hymn, she at last sinks among the fiery ruins. The whole incident is described with much spirit, and may not be inconsistent with manners and customs at some time prevalent in our country: it would, no doubt, have made the fortune of a common romance; but in such a work as *Ivanhoe*, it appears, I think, too glaring and meretricious, an ornament, and too much in the taste of the Miller and his Men.[12]

The concluding reference to Isaac Pocock's melodrama *The Miller and His Men* (1813) is telling for, although this particular playwright did not produce a version of Ivanhoe, he was responsible for adaptations of seven other novels including the enormously successful version of *Rob Roy* as *Rob Roy Macgregor; or Auld Lang Syne!* (first performed at Covent Garden on 12 March 1818).[13] Although he does not refer directly to the adaptations of Scott's work, Adolphus clearly associates it with stylistic tendencies that become more prevalent when the novels are transformed into stage plays. Thus Dibdin's early stage version of *Ivanhoe* makes full use of the melodramatic potential identified in the Ulrica episode as described by Adolphus when it requires a rousing spectacle to bring the second act of the play to a suitably exciting conclusion. The printed text of the play informs the reader that the

> *appartment gradually disappears; the castle is seen in flames; Ulrica appears exultingly on a lofty pinnacle; the Black Knight, Locksley, and Cedric, are fighting their way into the castle; Sir Brian carries off Rebecca, in spite of great opposition; Ulrica, brandishing her torch, sinks among the ruins, and in the midst of the tumult the act drop falls.* (p. 51)

This must indeed have presented a thrilling finale to the act: the distinct arrangement of different groups of protagonists, all simultaneously involved in separate but ultimately interrelated activities, creates a compelling and visually complex effect. One is perhaps reminded of Scott's observations, in relation to the French operatic version of *Ivanhoe*, about the 'skill' with which the actors 'are moved and grouped upon the stage'. However, such skills are held to be of little worth by Adolphus when he discusses the novels, and Scott himself berates the *Ivanhoe* opera for mangling his original story. The question that needs to be asked, then, is whether the dramatists were attracted to Scott's novels by what contemporary critics perceived to be their weaknesses rather than their strengths and that, as a result, they inevitably produced versions of the novels which were doomed to be judged as aesthetically inferior (as Scott claims they were).

In approaching this question, it is useful to begin by drawing attention to the use Adolphus makes of the generic category of the 'romance'. For Adolphus, Scott's novels are of a higher and more worthy classification than what he terms the 'common romance': the critical strategy here is one which attempts to differentiate the serious historical novel from more populist forms of prose fiction. More recently, Ian Duncan has argued that it is precisely Scott's use of the romance form that makes his novels distinctive and enables them to contribute significantly to the development of the British novel in the nineteenth century. Duncan notes Franco Moretti's observation that the English novel has failed to separate 'high' from 'low' literature and that the result has been a number of prominent 'synthetic' novelists who combine, or confuse, the elitist and the populist. Duncan proceeds to observe:

This morphological oddity nevertheless constitutes what is most power-ful in British fiction. Romance marks the novel's claim upon imaginative authenticity as the form of national life, appropriated by a middle-class hegemony ... from very different sources – from a popular culture of living speech and song and tale-telling, and from the literary culture of an aristocratic hegemony in the past. Official nationalism, 'the invention of tradition', no doubt represented a counter-revolutionary diversion of energies of protest and resistance; but at the same time it contained and expressed those energies, it kept them in circulation.[14]

If Scott is a 'synthetic figure' in this way then he is so because his work, according to Duncan, attempts to create an image of a unified nation through a synthesis of disparate and potentially oppositional elements. Of particular interest to the present discus-sion are those elements of 'popular culture' identified by Duncan: these are most readily the aspects of the (very wide-ranging) defini-tion of 'romance' which find analogies within popular melodrama. Duncan suggests that the novel, as used by Scott and others, is a 'counter-revolutionary' form deployed by a 'middle-class hegemony' to contain and control those discourses which might threaten their hegemonic power. He suggests that such appropria-tion none the less allows these competing, 'popular' discourses to continue to be expressed and kept in 'circulation'. Adaptations of the novels, however, would seem to recirculate Scott's appropria-tions in a decidedly different fashion. The 'common' element of the romance observed by Adolphus is allowed to come to the fore and the work of the (literary) novelist is recycled by playwrights like the author of *The Miller and His Men*. Denied the supporting framework of antiquarian exposition, the self-immolation of the defiant Ulrica reveals itself to full melodramatic effect. In returning to the question posed earlier, then, it would seem that issues of contemporary aesthetic taste need to be rearticulated in terms of the cultural classifications occasioned by changing ideologies of class and social status. In relation to *Ivanhoe* in particular, we need to be aware of the shifting representations of national identity inherent in the shifts from novel romance to stage melodrama.

However, before leaving the topic of the general, formal similar-ities and differences between the novel and the drama, it is instruc-tive to explore slightly further the fact that, in his comments about the operatic *Ivanhoe*, Scott should choose to draw attention to the way in which the production 'greatly mangled' his story. The opera (which was, in turn, adapted for English audiences by Michael Raphino Lacy as *The Maid of Judah; or Knights Templars* at Covent Garden in 1829) does indeed change the story considerably, but the comment is ironic coming, as it does, from a man whom contemporary reviewers often accused of mangling his own stories. In part, these reviewers were attacking Scott's plots for their unrealistic or illogical 'romance' elements which pay insufficient attention to the realism that they believed was required of the novel as a genre. As such they are contributing to a bourgeois tendency to limit and contain what Duncan terms the 'popular culture of living speech and song and tale-telling'. Yet, often, their criticisms are more thoroughgoing. The reviewer of a number of Scott novels in the October 1821 issue of the *Quarterly Review*, for example, registers with relief the fact that the popularity of *Rob Roy* renders unnecessary a retelling of the novel's story; he writes that 'we never rejoiced more in the circumstances which exempt us from endeavouring to relate our author's plots: for though we have this instant closed the last volume, and though one of the objects of our re-perusal was to make out the story, we are by no means sure that we have succeeded'.[15] Another reviewer, discussing *Ivanhoe* in the *Monthly Magazine* for February 1820, similarly complains that the novel exhibits 'the want of a good story',[16] and Scott himself, in the 'Introductory Epistle' to *The Fortunes of Nigel* confesses that he possesses what seems to be an inevitable inability to discipline himself to keep to the plot: 'Characters expand under my hand; incidents are multiplied; the story lingers, while the materials increase; my regular mansion turns out a gothic anomaly, and the work is complete long before the point I proposed.'[17] What makes this issue relevant to the topic of theatrical adaptation is that Scott viewed his self-acknowledged difficulties with plot structure as an aspect of his writing which precluded him from the composition of drama – as he writes in the 'Introductory Epistle', 'It may pass for one good reason for not writing a play, that I cannot form a plot'.[18]

The discussion so far has, therefore, identified two facets of Scott's writing: its penchant for what was termed 'melodramatic' effect, and its inability to control and contain a rambling and digressive plot. The first of these two traits would appear to render the novels attractive for writers who aspired to adapt them for the stage; the second would seem to present these playwrights with problems which would need to be addressed if they were to produce a play which had adequate coherence for dramatic representation. In considering the formal qualities of Scott's novels and the demands of the theatre in this way, it is instructive to call upon the influential work of Georg Lukacs who, in *The Historical Novel*, alerts us to the ideological implications of generic difference. Lukacs argues that both the historical novel and the historical drama aim to present what he calls 'a *total picture* of objective reality', but that they adopt different formal strategies in order to do this and that such strategies are intrinsically connected with the ideological imperatives of a specific historical moment.[19] For Lukacs the drama has what one might term a clarity of outline in that it focuses upon the collision of clearly defined representative individuals. He observes that 'the social collision, at the centre of drama, round which everything revolves and to which all components of the "totality of movement" refer, requires the portrayal of individuals, who in their personal passions directly represent those forces whose clash forms the material context of the collision'.[20] The result of this concentration upon isolated representative individuals leads to what Lukacs perceives to be one of the most important 'formal tendencies' of the drama, the 'singling out of the significant factors from the entire complex of reality, their concentration and the creation out of their connections of an image of life upon a heightened level'.[21] The novel, on the other hand, focuses not on individual representative figures but aspires to a more comprehensive and wide-ranging depiction of social diversity and multiplicity; it aims to create a 'thoroughly concrete, complex and intricate world inclusive of all the details of human behaviour and conduct in society'.[22] One result of such all-inclusiveness, one might argue, could be the loss of plot clarity as observed by Scott's contemporary critics: in place of simple dramatic 'collision' the historical novel offers a distinctive multiplication of incidents that Scott laments in the 'Introductory Epistle' but which, according to Lukacs, marks the innovative formal feature of the genre.

Although the contemporary critics, as has been seen, often bemoaned the lack of a clear plot outline in Scott's fiction, they did, none the less, respond positively to the 'concrete' world that the novels present. The reviewer in the *Quarterly Review* already quoted, writes of *Ivanhoe*:

> We have little to say about the story, but that it is totally deficient in unity of action, and consists, in fact, of a series of events, which occurred, at about the same time, to a set of persons who happened to be collected at the lists of Ashby. The associations, however, which are connected with the actors and the times, and the vividness of the narration prevent the interest from flagging – or rather renew it with each adventure – and the want of one concentrated interest may only make the different scenes more amusing, by allowing the reader leisure to pause and look round him as he passes.[23]

The criteria by which the writer judges Scott's failure at the level of 'story' are evidently derived, at least in part, from traditions of dramatic criticism ('it is totally deficient in unity of action'), but such quasi-dramatic shortcomings are seemingly more than compensated for by the ability of *Ivanhoe* to create a complex fictional world into which the reader is encouraged to enter via an imaginative involvement with the various 'scenes' that 'he' passes through. The 'one concentrated interest', that Lukacs would identify with the formal requirements of the drama might be missing, but it is clear that Scott's novels succeeded in delivering a satisfying alternative experience for contemporary readers. Having said this, Lukacs's generic scheme enables us to perceive potential ideological differences in the shift from one generic experience to another. For Lukacs, the novel's formal departure from the 'tragic collision' of drama is the result of an increasingly complex relationship between the bourgeois 'individual' on the one hand and 'society' on the other, in which each protagonist experiences their own private life as in large part independent of broader public movements. In addition, he notes that 'there are definite phases in the growth of society where the mutual blunting of contradictions is the typical form in which social antagonisms are decided'.[24] This conservative tendency within the novel as a genre is neatly illustrated by the specific example of *Ivanhoe* in which the creation of an 'English' identity is, as was suggested earlier, the result of a 'mutual blunting' of the Saxon, Norman and Jewish cultural identities which go together to form Scott's complex historical world.

If we return to the specific issue of adaptation, the question arises as to whether the formal requirements of a dramatic adaptation would have a tendency to reformulate such 'mutual blunting' in terms of a more polarised scene of conflict and opposition. If, as Lukacs suggests, 'tragic collision' in the drama reveals 'the most highly generalized features of revolutionary transformations in life itself, reduced to the abstract form of movement', then there is a potential for the relationship between novel and adaptation to be one between a socially conservative form on the one hand and a more socially confrontational mode on the other.[25] Lukacs is, of course, writing about tragedy rather than melodrama, but as Peter Brooks, amongst others, makes clear, melodrama too is crucially concerned with 'collision':

> The ritual of melodrama involves the confrontation of clearly identified antagonists and the expulsion of one of them. It can offer no terminal reconciliation, for there is no longer a clear transcendent value to be reconciled to. There is, rather, a social order to be purged, a set of ethical imperatives to be made clear.[26]

Whether tragedy or melodrama, therefore, one might expect the language of theatre to transform not simply the medium but also the ideological significance of Scott's original text. In the specific case study offered by the present chapter, it will be argued that *Ivanhoe*'s implicit and explicit exploration of English national identity is provided with new meanings through the differing cultural identities constructed through the generic reformulations of Scott's work. The next section will demonstrate how such meanings are generated even when the playwright apparently aspires to no more than a simple reworking of the original story of the novel.

IN HIS DISCUSSION OF THE essential differences between the drama and the novel, Georg Lukacs usefully quotes the opinions of Otto Ludwig on what would need to happen if a play were transformed into a novel or a novel into a play:

> This is the chief difference between the hero of the novel and the dramatic hero. If one were to think of *Lear* as a novel, then Edgar would probably have to be the hero. ... If, on the other hand, one wanted to

turn Rob Roy into a drama, then *Rob Roy* himself would have to be the hero, but the story would have to be considerably changed, Francis Osbaldistone would have to be omitted entirely. Similarly, in *Waverley* Vich Ian Vohr would have to be the tragic hero and in *The Antiquary* the Countess Glenallen.[27]

Lukacs quotes this passage to support his hypothesis that the dramatic hero is necessarily an embodiment of certain polarised forces which enter into conflict and collision with other such characters. In the novel, on the other hand, the hero is necessarily a more 'middle of the road' figure (to quote Lukacs's translators) who epitomises the novel's sense of complex compromise between extremes of passion and thought. Thus, in *Rob Roy*, the novel's hero is the essentially bourgeois Osbaldistone who remains a fairly passive and detached figure unwittingly caught up in a series of exciting Highland adventures. These adventures are ultimately of national importance, but Osbaldistone's marriage to Diana Vernon at the end of the novel can only rehearse at a private level the more public rapprochement that takes place in the political arena which provides the backdrop to the novel's central narrative. Ludwig and Lukacs argue that the novel's rather shadowy figure of Rob Roy would be a far more appropriate candidate for the role of hero in a dramatic version of Scott's tale. As a flamboyant character of public legend who embodies within himself the spirit of righteous revenge and hostility towards the usurpers of national prerogatives, Rob Roy represents far more obviously a form of polarised opposition.

On the whole, Lukacs and Ludwig offer a convincing line of argument, but it is, none the less, one which is problematised somewhat by the fact that Scott's novel is entitled *Rob Roy* rather than the more prosaic *Frank Osbaldistone*. The reason for the author's choice of title perhaps becomes clearer if one introduces the third generic term of the 'romance' as discussed by Ian Duncan: insofar as it is a romance, *Rob Roy* has an eponymous hero; insofar as it follows the novelistic trends defined by Lukacs, this larger-than-life protagonist has to be mediated through the moderating presence of Osbaldistone. Scott tempers the dangerously excessive tendencies of the Highland rebel by presenting them from the perspective of a more sober narrator whose sensibilities have a greater affinity with that of the novel's readership. During the course of the novel too, this narrator has to learn to control his own 'wayward' impulses (epitomised early on by filial disobedience and a desire to write extravagant verse romances) and become a more 'responsible' member of society. However, such a reading of the novel's formal strategies suggest a structural tension at its centre, a tension which might be brought to the fore in the action of a theatrical adaptation.

If one now returns to *Ivanhoe*, one can see that it too displays similar tensions. In may ways, of course, Ivanhoe might be interpreted as a relatively 'middle of the road' figure in that the more obviously important national disputes are played out between other characters of far greater public importance; characters, for example, such as King Richard and his brother Prince John. Having said this, Scott often seems intent on losing Ivanhoe behind the rich tapestry of antiquarian detail and busy characterisation which so many contemporary commentators defined as the novel's distinctive feature. As a disinherited child returning to prove his worth and fight for his personal autonomy (epitomised in his love for Rowena), Ivanhoe has the makings of a character of 'collision' rather than compromise. This potentially disruptive force of opposition is held in check by the fact that it is frequently placed in the background rather than the foreground of the circuitously unfolding narrative. Thus, for example, Ivanhoe's first appearance in the novel would seem to present him as an archetypal figure of romance. He appears in the forest in the guise of a pilgrim and offers his services as a guide to Prior Aymer and Brian de Bois-Guilbert who are lost on their way to Rotherwood. He is referred to throughout the scene as the 'stranger' and his provocative retorts to the already unamiable Prior and Knight Templar, together with his admission that he was 'born a native of these parts', alert the reader to the fact that he is not quite what he appears to be and that he is almost certain to play a more significant role in the narrative than his humble clothing implies.[28] Having established Ivanhoe's presence in the novel in this way, Scott then allows him to drift into the background. The next chapter provides a detailed introduction to Cedric and Rotherwood and it is only in the chapter which follows that the 'pilgrim' and fellow travellers enter the hall. Scott describes his pilgrim's garb and then allows him to take up a position of anonymity within the room:

He followed modestly the last of the train which entered the hall, and, observing that the lower table scarcely afforded room sufficient for the domestics of Cedric and the rest of his guests, he withdrew to a settle placed beside and almost under one of the large chimneys, and seemed to employ himself in drying his garments, until the retreat of some one should make room at the board, or the hospitality of the steward should supply him with the refreshments in the place he had chosen apart. (p. 56)

Such self-effacement, whilst working to create a sense of laudable modesty, also serves to efface Ivanhoe from the novel's action. Positioned apart from the other protagonists he remains 'invisible' to the reader and it is not until the next chapter, and the arrival of Isaac of York at Rotherwood, that the 'pilgrim' is again brought to the reader's attention when he offers Isaac his warm seat by the chimney (p. 65). Again his kindness creates a positive effect, but Scott has made no effort to remind the reader of his presence up until this point and, having made his kindly intervention, Ivanhoe retreats into the background and Scott continues with a detailed description of Isaac. Of course, what follows brings Ivanhoe sharply to the fore: there is a dispute about the valour of King Richard's knights in the Holy Land and Ivanhoe intervenes to great effect. The Templar replies to a question from Rowena about the role of the English army:

'Forgive me lady,' replied De Bois-Guilbert; 'the English monarch did, indeed, bring to Palestine a host of gallant warriors, second only to those whose breasts have been the unceasing bulwark of that blessed land.'

'Second to NONE,' said the Pilgrim, who had stood near enough to hear, and had listened to this conversation with marked impatience. All turned towards the spot from whence this unexpected asseveration was heard. 'I say,' repeated the Pilgrim in a firm and strong voice, 'that the English chivalry were second to NONE who ever drew sword in defence of the Holy Land ...' (p. 67)

This outburst could be said to mark Ivanhoe's real entry into the narrative: his disagreement with de Bois-Guilbert establishes an opposition which will only be resolved by the latter's death at the end of the novel. More immediately, Ivanhoe proceeds in the next chapter to rescue Isaac from the clutches of de Bois-Guilbert by an exciting night-time flight from Rotherwood. And yet, such flurries of activity are somewhat reminiscent of the way in which Scott presents the eponymous hero of *Rob Roy*. Like Rob Roy, Ivanhoe often acts to great effect and then disappears for large sections of the narrative whilst other characters take the foreground. Thus, after the hurried departure from Cedric's hall, Ivanhoe doesn't feature again until he appears in the lists at Ashby and, when he does appear, he is introduced as if from the perspective of various spectators in the crowd as the, again anonymous, 'Disinherited' Knight. Scott evidently works hard to frustrate the reader's direct engagement with Ivanhoe: if Rob Roy's oppositional temperament is mediated through the first-person narrative of Osbaldistone, then Ivanhoe's self-assertion is dissipated through the complexity of the interactions taking place within the society he inhabits.

It is tempting to call Ivanhoe's outburst at Rotherwood 'dramatic' and one can retrospectively appreciate how Scott's strategy of removing his hero from the eye of the reader enables them to share the shock of the gathered company when confronted with such an 'unexpected asserveration'. Yet after having created such an effect, Scott, as a novelist, is able to provide an insight into Ivanhoe's preceding emotions: '"Second to NONE," said the Pilgrim, who had stood near enough to hear, and had listened to this conversation with marked impatience.' Like the characters in the hall, the reader has not noticed the proximity of Ivanhoe to de Bois-Guilbert, nor has he or she witnessed Ivanhoe's increasing impatience. Unlike the characters in the novel, though, the reader is able to catch up on such information (without losing the 'dramatic' effect of the scene) through the controlling presence of an omnipresent narrator. However, the translation of this 'dramatic' scene in a novel into a dramatic scene upon the stage would create inevitable, and perhaps insurmountable, problems. Such problems lead back, as will be seen, to the distinctions discussed earlier in the present chapter between the dramatic hero on the one hand and the hero of the novel on the other.

The opening scene of Thomas Dibdin's *Ivanhoe; or, The Jew's Daughter* takes place in Cedric's 'rude Saxon Hall'. The scene begins with a short series of interactions between Wamba, Gurth and Cedric which provide a context for the action and offer information about, amongst other things, the fact that Ivanhoe has been disinherited by his already rather remorseful father. Music then sounds to accompany the entrance of 'the Prior Aymer, and Sir Brian, two Saracens and a Pilgrim' (p. 13). After a very brief exchange of greetings, music again sounds so herald the entry of Rowena. The stage direction reads: '*Music. Elgiva and six damsels precede the Lady Rowena, who after much ceremony is seated next Cedric, the Prior and the Knight on each side, the officers, &c. at a lower table, near them at a table by himself, the Pilgrim, whose face is concealed*' (p. 13). The 'pilgrim' enters and, as in the novel, he sits on his own away from the other characters. However, on stage this has the opposite effect to that created within the novel: Ivanhoe's isolation foregrounds his presence which is constantly before the audience. In some ways akin to the staging of Act I, Scene ii of *Hamlet*, in which the brooding prince in his suit of mourning is from the outset perceived to be at odds with the apparent complacency of the court, Ivanhoe in the present scene stands out as a potentially disruptive figure who is literally and metaphorically positioned on the margins of his society. The concealment of his face only serves to heighten an immediately established relationship between Ivanhoe and the other protagonists. He evidently does not wish to be recognised but his attempts at concealment only grant him an effective invisibility in relation to the other characters on stage. For the audience he gains, at the very least, an immediate identity as a person who is almost certainly known to the others and whose identity will in all probability be revealed as the action unfolds. Of course, the playwright also has to work with the assumption that many members of the audience will already have read Scott's novel (this is, after all, what lies behind the defensive introductory address discussed earlier). For such theatregoers, the 'pilgrim' is instantly recognisable as Ivanhoe and the pleasure of the scene lies in the anticipation of the outburst against Sir Brian which they know is to follow. Dibdin prepares for this outburst by carefully arranging his protagonists upon the stage. Shortly after the entrance of Rowena, the audience is introduced to Isaac:

(Music. Isaac enters, bows with great humility, all turn from him, he finds no seat, seems distressed and hurt.)

PILGRIM *(Rising)*: Old man my garments are dried, my hunger is appeased, thou art both wet and fasting.

(The Jew bows low, the Pilgrim places a cup and food before him, seems to refuse his thanks, and goes to the other end of the hall.)

SIR BRIAN: Pledge me mine host to those knights in arms, who bear them best in Palestine, as champions of the Cross, the templars, and knights of Saint John.

ROWENA: Were there none in the English army, whose names are worthy mention, besides those knights?

SIR BRIAN: King Richard's chiefs were second only to those warriors.

PILGRIM *(From a distance)*: Second to none! *(All look round.)* Aye! I repeat it. Second to none! (I.i, pp. 14–15)

Ivanhoe's interaction with Isaac refocuses the audience's attention and, perhaps even more explicitly than in the novel, isolates his act of generosity against the backdrop of his society's cruel anti-Semitism. The temporarily shared stage space of Jew and pilgrim visually emphasises their shared position as outcasts amongst those people gathered in the hall. Furthermore, in terms of stage-business, the interaction with Isaac enables Ivanhoe to move, as Sir Brian speaks, towards the other end of the stage. It will be remembered how, in the novel, Scott notes that Ivanhoe 'stood near enough to hear' the conversation taking place between de Bois-Guilbert and Rowena and, earlier, after offering Isaac his seat, Scott describes how 'without waiting the Jew's thanks, [he] went to the other side of the hall; – whether from unwillingness to hold more close communication with the object of his benevolence, or from a wish to draw near to the upper end of the table, seemed uncertain' (p. 65). In Dibdin's adaptation, Ivanhoe moves not towards the other speakers but away from them, the playwright's evident intention being to use the full width of the stage to create, visually, a sense of polarised opposition between Ivanhoe and Sir Brian. Both the scene from the novel and that from the play can be described as dramatic in effect, but only that from the play fully suggests the potential for the tragic collision of opposites that Lukacs claims is indispensable for the theatre. The important point to recognise in this example, however, is that Dibdin is providing what is, for the most part, a fairly 'faithful' adaptation. The changes to Scott's account are in many ways minimal and the shift in meaning that has been observed is, in part at least, brought about by the process of translation from what one might term one semiotic system to another. The necessary compression of action due to limitations of time and space, the inevitable exclusion of circumstantial detail and the necessity of characters being equally exposed to the potential gaze of the audience all work to transform the 'meaning' generated through the representation of Ivanhoe and his actions.

After the adventures at Rotherwood, the next action involving Ivanhoe in both Scott's novel and Dibdin's play takes place at the tournament at Ashby. Dibdin's adaptation presents the young knight's entry into the lists in the following fashion:

> (Trumpet sounds again; a young knight appears elegantly armed, on his shield is pourtrayed an oak tree pulled up by the roots; under it is the Spanish word, 'Desdichado,' or Disinherited. – He advances to the front, salutes the Prince and the ladies gracefully with his sword. Herald addresses him:)
>
> To which of these is thy defiance, knight?
>
> (The knight answers by signs.)
>
> WAMBA: If it be not to the smallest, my reputation, as a fool, is gone.
> HERALD: He defies all in turn; but chief Sir Brian.
>
> (The knight points to all, and then strikes Sir Brian's shield.)
>
> WAMBA: Then it is all over with all of us.
> REBECCA: I tremble for the youth.
> ISAAC: And I for the armour! 'Tis lost – all lost!
> PRINCE JOHN: Let them set forward!
>
> (Trumpets – after the usual ceremonies, they fight, Brian and the other knights are defeated, and retire.)
>
> PRINCE JOHN: Demand the stranger's name!
> HERALD: I have, my Lord; but he has made a vow for some certain season to disclose it; his title in the fields is 'The Disinherited'. (I.iv, p. 26)

In the novel, Ivanhoe appears at Ashby as, in effect, a 'new' character in that Scott describes his appearance from the perspective of the gathered spectators and thus gives no indication that the disinherited knight and the 'pilgrim' are one and the same person. This revelation has to wait until the end of the first day of the tournament. Although the drama also, necessarily, presents the knight from a spectator's viewpoint, Dibdin employs the dialogue between Rebecca and Isaac as a deliberate strategy to inform the audience that the knight they see is the pilgrim from the preceding scene. The singling out of Sir Brian as his major adversary in the combat which follows is thus a continuation of the heightened dramatic opposition that the playwright had established between these two protagonists earlier in the play. What is quite remarkable, though, is the fashion in which Dibdin insists on Ivanhoe's acts of communication all being conveyed either through the herald or, more significantly, through a series of dumbshows. In the novel, Ivanhoe speaks of his intentions and is also allowed to join in a mutually provocative exchange with de Bois-Guilbert before they engage in combat. The effect of the play is, therefore, very different and this difference is intimately involved with generic choice.

In the opening scene, the silence of the pilgrim is imbued with meaning insofar as the audience is aware of his oppositional presence on stage in a way that the reader of the book is not. Dibdin thus incorporates into his adaptation of the episode a sense of anticipation for the spoken outburst that follows and something similar is taking place during the scene at Ashby. In a discussion of early melodrama, Simon Shepherd and Peter Womack focus upon Barnabus Rayner's play *The Dumb Man of Manchester* (1837) in order to highlight key features of the genre. In this play, the hero Tom's dumbness prevents him from defending himself against a wrongful accusation of murder and he has to resort instead to the use of sign language. At one level, Shepherd and Womack suggest, this inability to speak foregrounds certain aspects of the melodrama's relationship with its audience:

> The audience's involvement with the drive of the *narrative* seems more important than its involvement with the situation of any one character. From its earliest days, the first English translators of French melodrama felt that their audiences wanted action rather than lengthy exposition in dialogue. Making the main character dumb is merely a hardline implementation of this formula. For it is not the complexity of Tom's character but the shape of his narrative that grips an audience.[29]

Part of this narrative strategy, so Shepherd and Womack suggest, is achieved by the fact that melodrama 'devises situations in which audiences know more than sympathetic characters'. In the present scene from Dibdin's play, the playwright implicitly calls upon the audience's prior knowledge of the *Ivanhoe* story by structuring the action around not simply the fight between Ivanhoe and Sir Brian, but also around the revelation of the knight's true identity. Prior to his arrival on stage it seems that no one is about to respond to trumpets calling for challengers to Prince John's knights. The following exchange takes place between Cedric and Rebecca:

> CEDRIC: No one to accept this challenge! must I in my old age put on my mail and hauberk?
> REBECCA: Oh, my lord, were your son, Ivanhoe, but here. (I.iv, p. 25)

Almost immediately after this, Gurth arrives to herald the arrival of the disinherited knight. The dramatic irony here is almost palpable – even those members of the audience who weren't previously aware of the shared identity of Ivanhoe, the pilgrim and the knight would develop a strong suspicion that this was indeed the case. As a melodrama, and also as an adaptation of a well-known book, Dibdin's *Ivanhoe* thrives on the kind of audience foreknowledge of events indicated by Shepherd and Womack. The present scene therefore creates a sense of audience anticipation which is dramatically fulfilled when, at the end, the wounded Ivanhoe attempts to crown Rowena 'queen of the day':

> *(Music. The knight, who seems exhausted, bows to the Prince, approaches Rowena with evident difficulty, and while attempting to salute with his sword, falls at her feet as if dead – they raise him, remove his helmet; he appears pale, wounded, and bleeding.)*
>
> ROWENA: 'Tis he! Tis Ivanhoe – dead – lost!
> CEDRIC: Now, Heaven forbid! My son! My son!
> ROWENA: 'Tis Ivanhoe!
>
> *(She faints in Cedric's arms. All form a tableau: and the act drop falls.)*
> (I.iv, p. 28)

This final speechless tableau both satisfies the audience's desire for the knight's identity to be revealed (and thus brings the characters on stage to the level of understanding already attained by the audience) and provides the starting point for another similar desire (for

Ivanhoe's 'death' to be revealed as a misunderstanding). Ivanhoe appears, then, not so much as a 'character' but rather as a form of 'plot function'; or, as Shepherd and Womack put it, performing 'a character successfully did not involve a search for coherence and unity but the creation of a succession of good pictures' and that these pictures were 'thrilling' because of 'their transformation into one another'.[30] The tableau at the end of the first act of *Ivanhoe* thus marks one narrative coordinate in the play's unfolding story, the dynamics of which depend quite considerably on dramatic elements in excess of simple speech and dialogue.

However, at another level, the silence and dumbshows of the disinherited knight work to suggest further degrees of audience involvement. Ivanhoe is silent because he cannot reveal his true identity; his lack of speech is effectively caused by his inability at this point in the narrative to declare who he is. The audience, knowing (or suspecting) who he is, experience his frustration and share his desire to speak out. Working from their reading of Rayner's *The Dumb Man*, Shepherd and Womack see such frustration as central to the melodramatic experience:

> Being able to acclaim the truth is the opposite of being trapped into a false truth. Melodrama may be said to construct excitement out of the possible alternation between being trapped by circumstances and being able to change them. … Melodrama's excitement may be said to relate to a fantasy of *agency*, the possibility of being able single-handedly to challenge authority and change it.[31]

From the present brief analysis of the first act of Dibdin's *Ivanhoe*, it can be seen that by foregrounding Ivanhoe as a figure of opposition within a narrative which relies more on action and visual display than authorial comment or character motivation and interiority, the play can be said to create this sense of 'agency' far more powerfully than the novel. Indeed, in Scott's novel, the possibility of individuals changing the world in which they live seems to be ruled out by his vision of a world shaped by apparently more complex social interactions which ultimately result in gradual change through consolidation and compromise. This is not to suggest that Dibdin's play is necessarily 'radical' in its tendencies. What is suggested, however, is that adaptation into another genre can offer the potential for different ideological nuances to be revealed in what appears to be a version of the same 'story'. Such potential becomes more overt when Scott's *Ivanhoe* is adapted by George Soane as *The Hebrew*.

THE OPENING ADDRESS TO Dibdin's play seems to suggest that the model of adaptation proposed by the playwright aspires to no more than an attempt at a 'literal' transfer of 'scenes' from one genre to another. However, not all adaptations of the time were so tentative. George Soane's adaptation of *Ivanhoe* as *The Hebrew. A Drama, In Five Acts*, which was first performed on 2 March 1820, seems to have more ambitious aspirations. In the Prologue to the play, provided by a Mr Barlow, the audience is told that Dibdin has lit his 'torch obscure' at Scott's 'shrine':

> yet he, alas! unfit,
> The scenes of 'Ivanhoe' to copy here,
> Hath sought for safety in a humbler sphere.
> If from compiler's dull mechanic ways,
> He fearless turns, will *you* withhold your praise?[32]

The message here would seem to be ambiguous. On the one hand, Soane is presented as being inferior in artistic talent to the novelist whose work he is adapting. Unlike Dibdin, who claims to have 'copied' at least some of the 'scenes' of *Ivanhoe* in his adaptation, Barlow's Prologue suggests that such transcription is beyond the ability of anyone not possessing the genius of the original novelist. Immediately after this statement, however, such acts of simple duplication are referred to as no more than the work of a 'compiler's dull mechanic ways'. This would seem to suggest that the playwright who aims to achieve no more than a 'faithful' rendition of the novel is lacking in any individual creative ability. To turn away from such a model of adaptation is therefore to engage in a more imaginative activity which aspires to an element of original creativity through the process of generic transformation.

In keeping with this suggestion of a more ambitious understanding of the act of adaptation, the Prologue to *The Hebrew* can, both directly and indirectly, be seen to attempt to establish a more complex relationship than is to be found in the Prologue to Dibdin's *Ivanhoe* between issues of genre on the one hand and broader social and political concerns on the other. The speech begins with a comparison between society in contemporary England and that of the England described in Scott's novel (and the play about to be performed). This comparison quickly modulates into a reflection upon the current political situation caused by the death of George III in the January of 1820:

> In these blest days, the horrid din of arms
> No longer wakes us with its dread alarms; –
> Our warriors seek no more the field or flood,
> And men have leisure to be wise and good.
> Yet we, alas! have scarcely dried the tear,
> Which flow'd to consecrate a monarch's bier; –
> Who, for those laurels watch'd through years of gloom,
> Which only rose to decorate his tomb. –
> Whate'er the factions of our giddy throng,
> Whatever ills from public woes have sprung;
> The veriest wretch that owns a Briton's name,
> Had prov'd his shield – the bulwark of his fame. (Prologue, p. 7)

The attitude towards the past here is, to say the least, ambiguous. The wisdom and goodness which derives from 'leisure', whilst evidently more pleasurable than the horrors of war, are implicitly found to be less potentially honourable than the glory of fighting for one's monarch or one's country. The image of George III rather awkwardly mediates between past and present. On the one hand he was far from being the ideal king of chivalric romance: incapacitated by a debilitating mental illness, he was a king in name only and could do no more than dream of the 'laurels' of which the heroic monarch should be worthy. On the other hand, the national grief for a deceased monarch is called upon to assert a country which is unified in its mourning and which would have been prepared, if the occasion had arisen, to support their monarch with a show of (chivalric) arms. None the less, this unity exists only precariously within the speech, for it is established in and against the rather unsettling context of 'factions' and 'public woes'.

As if the discussion of the present state of Britain is too painful for contemplation, the speaker turns from the topic abruptly and addresses himself to the play about to be performed. Despite the change in topic, the troubling tension between past and present continues:

> No more! – forgive the bard these mournful strains,
> Our '*Hebrew*' of to-night attention claims: –
> No longer scoff'd, in peaceful compact blend
> *Christian* and *Jew*, by turns each other's friend. –
> The days of yore are past, the advent'rous times,
> When men were great in virtues as in crimes; –
> Such days have left us, yet one master hand,
> Hath borne the spell, they rise at his command;
> Triumphant genius bids the past appear,
> To wake our terrors or command the tear; –
> Unlike the bards or old who hapless pin'd
> In want and solitude, your voice combin'd,
> Pours the rich bounty of your just applause, –
> The *Novelist's*, your own, and virtue's cause. (Prologue, p. 7)

The speaker establishes an immediate contrast between past and present through the contemporary harmony of Christian and Jew. Whether such harmony existed or not, it functions again as an only partially effective counter to the factions and woe which the speaker has already gestured towards in contemporary society. In anticipating the play to come, the astute spectator might expect some displacement of present disunity on to past racial tension. Moreover, the speech indicates that the disharmony and villainy of the past was also complemented by a counteracting greatness which belonged to earlier 'advent'rous' times and is no longer present in nineteenth-century Britain. As elsewhere, there is an awkward slippage between a celebration of social progress and a lament for cultural decline.

Out of this confusion Walter Scott emerges as the 'one master hand' who, whilst he is able to recreate the adventurous nature of the past, is, as a writer, distinct from his predecessors and a product of a clearly modern society. The speech provides a recognisably 'Romantic' image of previous writers pining in 'want and solitude' before presenting Scott as a modern novelist whose 'rich bounty' is both the critical esteem and, crucially, the financial reward that are implied by popular success. Yet the choice of the word 'applause' to signify this success resonates interestingly and significantly within the present dramatic context as it implies that the speech addresses its audience in the theatre as if it is synonymous with the book-buying public. It is, of course, quite probable that many theatregoers were also individual readers who had bought and read Scott's novels. However, to read the speech's rhetoric in terms of individuals is to miss the full complexity of the generic and social issues to which it gives rise. Theatre audiences and the readers of novels are not synonymous as types, although individuals might very well belong to both groups. In terms of nineteenth-century cultural history, the mass-public readership of popular novels was a new social phenomenon and the rhetorical strategy of the speech is to represent this phenomenon in terms of a more traditional image of an audience in the theatre. What the speech effectively provides is an image of the theatre audience as a metaphor for the novel-reading public and, as such, the 'real' theatre audience can only be addressed as the vehicle of this metaphor rather than its tenor. The far larger and differently constituted novel readership lies beyond an audience that can be addressed and influenced by the dramatist and thus the certainty of the speech's second-person speech forms ('your voice combined ... your own and virtue's cause') is undercut by the fact that the dramatist is only able to communicate with a mere representation of the vaguely defined grouping he wishes to address.

The dramatist and the contemporary novelist are different kinds of writer and their 'audiences' are different in form even if they have some congruence in membership. The problem takes on a broader significance within the Prologue to *The Hebrew* because the speech attempts to imply a national and political unity which is arrived at through a shared aesthetic sensibility:

> If from compiler's dull mechanic ways,
> He fearless turns, will *you* withhold your praise?
> Ah, no! who boldly dares will ever find,
> A *British* audience, even in censure kind (Prologue, p. 7)

The 'audience' is here addressed as a quintessentially British entity which defines and is defined by certain national characteristics. Such an appeal is evidently in keeping with the underlying theme of the creation of an English national identity in Scott's *Ivanhoe* and, the theatre audience would expect, the play they are about to watch. However, the implicit bifurcation of the 'audience' into traditional theatre spectators and more modern readers of novels would suggest that the certainty of a single, unified 'British audience' is called into question. Dramatist and novelist, play and novel, audience and readership are all brought together and yet separated within this Prologue and the problematic defining term seems to be that of national or cultural identity. As has been seen, the speech opens with an implicit appeal for unity at a time of national mourning, but it is an appeal which is subtly undercut by the admission of 'factions' and 'public woes'. The swerve to aesthetic considerations only serves to displace such issues elsewhere. The novelist and the dramatist both appeal to a 'British' audience – but there is no guarantee that either the 'audience' or the notion of what constitutes a British national identity are the same in both cases.

In his reading of Scott's *Ivanhoe*, John Sutherland suggests that the plot of the novel can be interpreted as an 'elegant compliment' to the Prince Regent which reflects the 'current condition of England in 1819', in which the nation suffers from the lack of a competent monarch but is none the less aware of a 'masterful heir-presumptive in the wings waiting to sweep in like the black knight and rescue his country from scheming politicos'.[33] For Sutherland, one of the most disturbing aspects of this nationalist fable is what he terms Scott's 'legitimation of anti-Semitic stereotypes' in his depiction of Isaac and Rebecca.[34] He notes that, even if he himself were not a 'racist', 'there is a consistent undercurrent of derogation in Scott's narrative which verges on the anti-Semitic' and observes in particular how, at the end of the novel, 'Isaac and Rebecca are made to leave the country: they are banished, presumably as racial contaminants'.[35] Against this reading of *Ivanhoe* as effectively advocating a version of ethnic cleansing, one can place the interpretation offered by Michael Ragussis which argues for a more generous and, indeed, a more complex treatment of race issues. Ragussis suggests that, at one level, the novel attempts to depict an evolution of English national identity based upon racial interaction rather than exclusion: 'In this way, Scott is able to define "England" as the product of racial and cultural mixture – neither as the simple preservation of the Saxon past in the face of Norman invasion, nor as the simple conversion of the Saxons into Normans.'[36] However, at another level Ragussis claims that Scott reveals the fissures within this conservative narrative of racial and cultural compromise and that he does this most obviously in his presentation of Isaac and, especially, Rebecca. Of the latter, he writes that she 'is of course the first erotic power that neither Ivanhoe nor Rowena can exorcise. But more than this, she is the blot on the conscience of England insofar as she represents the religious and racial question that England cannot solve.'[37] What for Sutherland is the banishment of anti-Semitism, then, is for Ragussis a contrived narrative dissonance which gives the lie to the English nationalist myth. Yet, whilst this reading is both suggestive and largely convincing, it fails to give adequate weight to the stereotypical presentation of Isaac by the narrator. He is introduced to the reader in a less than wholly positive fashion:

> His features, keen and regular, with an aquiline nose, and piercing black eyes; his high and wrinkled forehead, and long grey hair and beard, would have been considered handsome, had they not been the marks of a physiognomy peculiar to a race, which, during those dark ages, was alike detested by the credulous and prejudiced vulgar, and persecuted by the greedy and rapacious nobility, and who, perhaps, owing to that very hatred and persecution, had adopted a national character, in which there was much, to say the least, mean and unamiable. (p. 64)

Whilst there is an evident attempt here to depict the anti-Semitic bigotry and violence which the Jews had to endure, Scott none the less presents the 'mean and unamiable' Jewish stereotype as a 'truth' rather than as an offensively racist slur. As Anne Aresty Naman has suggested, it would seem that, whatever Scott's intentions, the result is 'an ambiguous attitude rather than a totally sympathetic one'.[38] In its ambiguities and irresolutions, *Ivanhoe*, to use Ian Duncan's words, 'continues to register the pressure of the categories – sexuality and race – that will mark the limits of "culture", the fluid space of national identity formation, in nineteenth-century discourse'.[39]

As regards the portrayal of Rebecca, Duncan notes that many readers have in fact been so attracted to her character that there has been a strong narrative desire for Ivanhoe to marry her rather than

Rowena and, in a footnote, he cites Soane's *The Hebrew* as an example of a subsequent version which 'contrives' such a union.[40] Yet the contrivance is far more thoroughly incorporated into the play's narrative than Duncan's brief account suggests. The play opens with a dialogue between Cedric and his son who is disguised as a 'Palmer' and who attempts to raise the topic of his own disinheritance:

> PALMER: My story is of Ivanhoe –
> CEDRIC *(interrupting him)*: My son! A father's curse, –
> PALMER: Curse not thy son.
> CEDRIC: I do.
> PALMER: Curse not thy son, old man; – he loves thee well.
> CEDRIC: It has not seem'd so; I will tell thee, Palmer;
>   Thou art a Saxon, and wilt understand me.
>   He lov'd a Jewess – that was sin enough;
>   He did deny to leave her at my bidding;
>   That was a sin a father could not pardon;
>   I banish'd him my house, my blood, the land. (I.i, p. 10)

From the very start of the drama, therefore, Ivanhoe's position as disinherited outcast is associated with the analogous situation of Isaac and Rebecca. The father's act of casting his son from the family 'house' has repercussions at the level of race ('blood') and national identity ('land'). In Act III, Scene i, Cedric reinforces this when he again banishes his son, who has by this time revealed his true identity, for refusing to give up Rebecca, with the threat that he will become a 'stranger to my home, my heart, my race' (p. 33). At the end of the second act, Wamba rushes on stage to inform Robin Hood and his men about the revelation of Ivanhoe's identity at the 'tourney', but in his excitement he confuses this news with that of Prince John's treatment of Isaac. As a result, he cryptically declares that 'the Jew turn'd out to be Ivanhoe – No – Ivanhoe turn'd out to be the Jew' (p. 29). As so often with the fool's pronouncements, this reveals a truth that is missed by his immediate audience for, at an important level of this adaptation, the audience in the theatre is asked to acknowledge the shared status of these two protagonists. Moreover, Soane's choice of title for the play clearly indicates a shift in focus: in terms of narrative importance and centrality, the Jew really does turn out to be Ivanhoe.

This centrality is registered from very early on in the first scene of the play. As in the novel, Ivanhoe, disguised as the Palmer, gives up his place by the fire to Isaac but, when Brian de Bois-Guilbert berates him for this, it is Isaac who replies with a retort about de Bois-Guilbert's defeat 'in combat with the young Ivanhoe' (p. 13). Thus Isaac has taken Ivanhoe's place as the main figure of opposition to the bigotry represented by de Bois-Guilbert and within this scene, and the play in general, he is allowed to voice his own racially and culturally specific grievances in a way that he is not in the novel:

BRIAN: Forth! Forth!
ISAAC: I pity thee;
   The poor old Jew – the dog – worse if worst be,
   Whom thy scorn spits upon, thy hatred loathes,
   Doth pity thee! think, Christian, what thou art,
   When one so poor, so beaten, so forlorn,
   Can say, I pity thee
BRIAN: Die villain!
CEDRIC: Hold!

Cedric keeps back Brian, who had drawn upon Isaac.

ISAAC: Oh, valour nobly shown, and wise as noble!
   For is it not a valour most discreet,
   That knows to safely choose its foe, and makes
   Its secure war on hands that lack the sword,
   Or swords that lack the hand?
BRIAN: Unloose me, sirs.
ISAAC: Hark how the lion roars!
PALMER: No more, old man.
PRIOR: Go forth, I say.
ISAAC: But this, and I am gone.
PRIOR: Be wise, and fear.
ISAAC: What should I fear? I've broke
   The bread of Cedric; – drank his wine – I'm safe
   In hospitality.
CEDRIC: 'Tis true; – He stays.
BRIAN: Thou money-bag – thou thing, whose Midas-touch
   Turns all to gold, –
ISAAC: And what art thou? – A cypher,
   That swells the social number though itself
   Is merely nothing. What seed hast thou sown?

What harvest reap'd? – What things of profit made?
What merchandize exchang'd? Thou hast set up
A false god, Honour, at whose shrine man's blood
Is pour'd in sacrifice by night and day;
Thy worship is a murder; – and thy life
Is nothing but that worship.

CEDRIC: Jew, no more.

ISAAC: I was too rash – Say 'twas the fault of age,
And pardon it; the dryest wood is still
The quickest to the spark. (I.i, pp. 13–14)

Not only does Isaac here have the opportunity to launch a ferocious attack upon the false 'honour' of the chivalric code adopted by de Bois-Guilbert, he is also allowed to defend his own economic activity in terms which accentuate its positive contribution to the national economy. The bitter irony comes from the fact that it is the social outsider who reveals the Norman presence to be a destructive 'cypher' within the social and economic fabric of England. The greedy usury of the stereotypical Jew is transformed into a socially useful activity and, elsewhere in the play, Soane is careful to establish that Isaac's human kindness overrides his desire for financial gain. (Unlike the novel, for example, in the play it is Isaac himself who refuses payment for the loan of the horse and armour to Ivanhoe in gratitude for the knight having saved his life). In the present scene, although Isaac's anger – and contempt – are self-evident, he is also portrayed as aspiring to an (ironically 'Christian') sense of pity and forgiveness. This tendency is perhaps displayed most graphically at the end of the third act where Isaac initially gloats over the apparently mortally wounded de Bois-Guilbert who, before he was hit by an arrow, was about to torture him:

ISAAC: Triumph! – he falls – How, – do my curses wound?
Dost thou not feel them griping at thy heart?
Christian, dost thou hear me?
Thine was the eagle's flight, – high, – high in air!
Thou lookst upon the sun, and in thy pride
Made it no shame to tear with rav'nous beak,
The birds of humbler quarry! – What thy wing
Is broken, flapping bloodily in dust –

May it ne'er heal again to bear thee up,
Where thou may'st souse upon the weaker things
That fly beneath thee – no – shame, Isaac, shame
List to his groans – list to the bubbling blood –
How his limbs quiver – Christian – I forgive thee.
END OF THE THIRD ACT (p. 41)

The transition from anger to forgiveness is here, as earlier, awkwardly managed: it is too abrupt to be psychologically convincing and appears almost tokenistic, a recognition of the 'correct' behaviour for a sympathetic character. And yet, given the fact that a theatre audience did not necessarily desire psychological realism, the foregrounding of Isaac's anger at the expense of supposedly more worthy feelings creates a situation in which spectators are encouraged to share the venom which results from Isaac's social alienation whilst their conscience is appeased by the introduction of the final note of forgiveness. In general, Isaac's anger is justified and it is this which fuels the audience's identification with him: he speaks with a nineteenth-century sense of injustice against the tyranny of arbitrary power. As Anastasia Nikolopoulou has argued in relation to other melodramatic adaptations of Scott novels, the melodramatist removed 'the life of the characters out of the historical forces controlling their actions and gave them a chance, if not to reach tragic heights, at least to confront their opponents in the flesh, even if they failed in the attempt'.[41]

William Hazlitt saw Soane's play at Drury Lane together with the adaptation of *Ivanhoe* by Samuel Beazley at Covent Garden and reviewed them both in the *London Magazine* for April 1820. His response to *The Hebrew* is interestingly ambivalent:

As a play, it is ill-constructed, without proportion or connection. As a poem, it has its beauties, and those we think neither mean nor few. It is disjointed, without dramatic decorum, and sometimes even to a ludicrous degree ... But notwithstanding this weakness in the general progress of the story there are individual touches of nature and passion, which we can account for in no other way so satisfactorily as by imagining the author to be a man of genius ...[42]

Hazlitt is attempting to distinguish between *The Hebrew*'s qualities as a performed text and as a text which is read: he refers directly to the printed version of the play in his review and states that he wishes to consider it as a 'literary composition' as well as a dramatic piece for the theatre. It is in this light that one can initially understand his distinction between a 'poem' and a 'play' in the above quotation. What Hazlitt seems to be claiming is that Soane's work succeeds as closet drama but not as performance. However, the issue is not quite so straightforward as this would suggest, for Hazlitt's grounds for complaint seem to be rooted in rather 'literary' principles of dramatic unity and 'decorum' which might, indeed, be antithetical to what Shepherd and Womack call the 'mixed' mode of the melodrama.[43] The 'closet' text of *The Hebrew* is successful for Hazlitt because of its frequent but isolated 'touches of nature and passion' which he describes in literary or poetic terms rather than as dramatic in the literal sense. Having said this, it is clear from elsewhere in the review that the critic also responded to such moments during the performance itself, specifically those aspects of the performance which involved the character of Isaac as embodied in the powerful stage presence of Edmund Kean:

> Upon the whole, this character, compared to the rough draught [*sic*] in the novel, is like a curiously finished miniature, done after a bold and noble design. For the dark, massy beard, and coarse weather-beaten figure, which we attribute to Isaac of York, we have a few sprinkled grey hairs, and the shriveled, tottering frame of the Hebrew; and Mr Kean's acting in it, in several places, was such as to terrify us when we find from the play-bills that he is soon to act Lear. Of the two plays, we would then recommend our readers to go to see Ivanhoe at Covent Garden: but for ourselves, we would rather see the Hebrew a second time at Drury Lane ...[44]

Here, Hazlitt's 'literary' judgement and his appreciation of dramatic effect pull him in opposite directions: Beazley's *Ivanhoe* is the better play according to established critical criteria, but *The Hebrew* is evidently the most compelling theatrical event. Indeed, such is the power of the performance that it seems to offer the spectator a more 'finished' rendition of Isaac than the mere draft version provided by Scott in his original novel; the play develops Isaac as a protagonist in ways which, although perhaps unexpected, seem, retrospectively, entirely convincing.

What Hazlitt specifically notes about Soane's extension of Isaac's role, and Kean's performance of it, is the element of terror they generate and also, implicitly, the echoes of *King Lear* they evoke. Anastasia Nikolopoulou suggests that melodrama fails to allow its protagonists to 'reach tragic heights', but it is clear that, whilst *The Hebrew* often deploys melodramatic strategies, it aspires to something akin to tragic status in its portrayal of Isaac and that this, as Hazlitt suggests, is indicated through Soane's conscious reworking of *King Lear*. Like Lear, Isaac is a man more sinned against than sinning, who possesses what Hazlitt recognised as the terrifying capacity to lay curses upon his tormentors. At the climax of the first act, after having escaped the machinations of de Bois-Guilbert with the aid of the 'palmer', Isaac draws upon an awareness of an extra-societal sense of justice. De Bois-Guilbert spurns Isaac's attempts at reconciliation:

ISAAC: Accept my hand.
BRIAN: Accept my vow of hate.
   Where now I would have taken grains of gold,
   I will have tons; Look to it, Jew.
PALMER: Indeed!

Violent storm.

ISAAC: Hark! how the tempest roars! Does not its voice
   Chide thy vain savage boasting? Does not feel
   Another world is clipping thee about?
   The howling wind makes faint thy loudest cries!
   The thunder shows thee as a sickly babe
   Screaming weak anger! – Hark! how it shakes these walls!
   While thy poor breath will scarcely move a rush.

A violent burst of wind beats open the window, and shows the blighted arm of an oak.

ISAAC: Ha! see yon blasted oak that flings its arm
   Across the window – Once that arm was stout –
   Ay, stouter than thine own – Proud earthworm, look! –
   Behold! – as that once was, so hast thou been; –
   As that is now, so shalt thou be –
   (To the Palmer)   Come! Come!

The Palmer and Isaac go out. Brian remains as if stupified.
END OF ACT I (I.iii, p. 21)

In many ways, Isaac's access to the quasi-divine justice of 'another world' informs the logic of the play's narrative structure. The dreadful prophecy voiced by Isaac at the end of this first act comes to fruition at the end of the play when de Bois-Guilbert meets his death before the anticipated combat with Ivanhoe can take place. His death is, of course, similar in the novel, but Soane makes a few telling alterations. In Scott's *Ivanhoe*, the author gives an unambiguously psychological explanation for the Templar's sudden death: 'Unscathed by the lance of his enemy, he had died a victim to the violence of his own contending passions.' The only suggestion of divine intervention is provided by the rather questionable authority of the Grand Master, who declares that, 'This is indeed the judgment of God' (p. 490). In *The Hebrew*, on the other hand, the death is explicitly associated with heaven's vengeance:

IVANHOE: Why dost thou droop thy sword?
BRIAN: What light was that
  Which shot across my face – I am withered – blasted;
  I've sin'd against earth and heaven – I die –

Brian reels: his Squire catches him in his arms and unclasps his Helmet.

ISAAC: Lo! heaven's wrath,
  The strong one is struck down! though helm and mail
  Tremble proud dust! your arms avail ye not,
  Pow'r clips ye as the air, felt though unseen. (V.iii, p. 65)

At one level, therefore, the play suggests a divine scheme of justice which militates against oppression and tyranny and allows the weak and outcast to regain their proper position within society. The death of de Bois-Guilbert paves the way for the marriage of Ivanhoe and Rebecca and an apparent resolution to the play's destructive social conflicts.

However, as in *King Lear*, no such resolution is possible in Soane's play and the final impression is one of lamentation rather than celebration. As Isaac's treatment by society becomes increasingly unbearable, his curses become increasingly nihilistic. No longer aimed at specific, guilty individuals, the curses evoke an image of complete devastation produced by a complete lack of hope. Learning of Rebecca's death sentence at the end of the fourth act, Isaac recalls Lear as he calls upon supernatural forces not for aid but for destruction:

> *Isaac holding his daughter to his breast, and stretching his right hand to Heaven.*
>
> ISAAC: Ye powers of air!
> Come to my breast – and now send forth your storms;
> Crush, crush us all to dust! one common tomb!
> Wind! lightning! thunder! blow! blaze! and strike!
> END OF ACT IV (V.iii, p. 53)

This evocation of universal death is extended to the opening scene of the final act which is set during a 'violent storm' in the 'Jew's Burying Ground'. Clearly modelled upon the storm scenes in *King Lear*, Isaac wrestles with his sanity, pitifully declaring, 'I am not mad – no – no – I am not mad' (V.i, p. 54). Existing on the borders between life and death, sanity and madness, this scene marks Isaac's position as one on the margins of the world which he inhabits. The Jew's Burying Ground provides a locus of exclusion and alienation, literally and figuratively on the outskirts of Christian society. Whereas Lear on the Heath has the consolation of rediscovered human contact, Isaac in the Burying Ground is only confronted with his own social isolation.

After such a bleak vision, any simple resolution to the play's social conflicts is impossible. Rebecca, unlike Cordelia, might be saved from death, but her father's fate is sealed:

> REBECCA: Art thou ill,
>   Dear father?
> ISAAC: Give me thy hand!
> REBECCA: 'Tis here.
> ISAAC: Where? – Where?
> REBECCA: You hold it now.
> ISAAC: Fear not my love:
>   'Tis but the first gush of exceeding joy.
>
> *Isaac starts from the arms of those who hold him, and gazes for a moment at his Daughter.*
>
> ISAAC: My child, wilt not, wilt not, to these old arms?
> REBECCA: Oh my dear father! *(Falls into his arms)*

ISAAC: Earth recedes – ah now
  I feel the presence of another world;
  The heavens unclasp their gates of burning light,
  The seat of immortality's unveil'd
  Where the great mover beams mid'st angel hosts;
  A sun 'midst untold stars – 'Tis sweet to die.

*Isaac sinks into the arms of Ivanhoe: Rebecca kneels grasping her
father's hand: the Curtain slowly falls to a plaintive melody.*
THE END (V.iii, p. 65)

Whilst Isaac's 'sweet' death contrasts with the somewhat bleaker
conclusion of *King Lear*, it is none the less upon a 'plaintive' rather
than a joyous note that the play concludes. It will be remembered
how Michael Ragussis has argued for the importance of the disso-
nant effect caused by Rebecca's exile at the end of Scott's novel. In
The Hebrew, Soane accentuates such dissonance by excluding his
play's hero from the harmonious reconciliations which certain
aspects of the narrative appeared to promise. Like Rebecca, according to Ragussis's reading of *Ivanhoe*, but with a far more
pronounced effect, Isaac here acts as a pointed reminder of the
violent exclusions upon which images of national and cultural unity
are established. There is indirect evidence to suggest that contemporary audiences found such a vision difficult or unpleasant to
assimilate. A contemporary review in the *London Magazine; and
Monthly Critical and Dramatic Review*, notes that 'on the first
representation of this piece, *Isaac* died, from excess of emotion, on
the delivery of his daughter. This has since been altered, and he does
not die; he pronounces, however, his dying speech, which is an
inconsistency, productive of a very bad effect.'[45] This, rather unfor-
tunate, change was presumably introduced in response to adverse
early audience reaction. As such it suggests the extent to which
Soane had succeeded in winning support and sympathy for Isaac as
a social outsider. The fact that his death was too painful for the
audience to acknowledge suggests the quasi-tragic status to which
Scott's marginal figure had been elevated.

In his discussion of what he takes to be Scott's implicit racism,
John Sutherland suggests that the novelist's treatment of race
should be read in connection with the polygenic theories of contemporary writers such as Robert Knox. Polygeny focused upon the

physical differences of ethnic groups and argued for the 'purity' of the origins of the major races. Whilst Scott might argue for the blending of Norman and Saxon in the formation of an English racial and cultural identity, he none the less espouses what Sutherland sees as a Knoxian hierarchical relationship between 'light' and 'dark' races. Thus the villains of the novel (and Isaac, of course) are all dark and swarthy, whereas the heroes and heroines are all fair skinned, fair haired and blue eyed. Unlike such polygenic beliefs, monogenic theories argued for a shared origin for all races. In contrast to the colonising and racist tendencies of polygeny, Sutherland notes that monogeny 'lent itself as a political ideology to philanthropic movements, such as abolitionism'.[46] It has been seen how, in *The Hebrew*, Soane plays down the racial stereotypes that are found in *Ivanhoe*. Moreover, from very early on, Soane establishes what, in Sutherland's terms, can be seen as a monogenic principle. In the first scene, when de Bois-Guilbert is racially abusing Isaac, Ivanhoe, in the guise of the palmer, springs to his defence:

BRIAN *(Contemptuously)*:　　　　And who art thou?
PALMER: I am – the Palmer; one who, in the lack
　　Of thy philosophy, thinks man is man,
　　Whate'er his faith, his habit, or his speech.
　　Come, Jew, I'll be thy safety. (I.i, p. 13)

This speech acts as a touchstone for the moral philosophy that informs the play as a whole and it is a philosophy which is in marked contrast to that presented within *Ivanhoe*. At a significant level, *The Hebrew* is uninterested in the larger political and cultural manoeuverings of Scott's novel: King Richard does not make an appearance and, although he is mentioned by a number of characters in the course of the action, his existence (or the political world he represents) does not feature in the play's conclusion. The reason for this would seem to be that notions of a rigidly enforced national identity work counter to the belief that 'man is man' whatever his race or creed. In *The Hebrew*, any myth of national unity is either false, or destructive, or both.

In 1820, with the death of George III and the accession of the Prince Regent to the throne as George IV, questions of national unity were very much in the air and the theatre played a significant role in contemporary debate. One of the most extravagant, and popular, contributions was staged at Drury Lane (like *The Hebrew*) from August of that year and ran for a remarkable 104 performances. The show in question was quasi-documentary reenactment of the coronation of George IV, lavishly put on with over four hundred actors and a stage replica of Westminster Abbey and Hall. Marilyn Gaull describes this extravaganza as:

> a gorgeous, opulent, patriotic, timely, and convincing representation of the peaceful transfer of power, the survival of ceremony, and the strength of tradition, an affirmation of the right of a remarkably decadent aristocracy to enjoy its privileges untouched by the democratic revolutions that were transforming societies all over the western world.[47]

'The Coronation' sits comfortably alongside *Ivanhoe* in its celebration of the 'strength of tradition', particularly if one recalls Sutherland's suggestion that Scott's novel constituted an 'elaborate compliment' to the then Prince Regent. And yet, on the same stage only a few months earlier, *The Hebrew* played to a similar audience and had conveyed a starkly different message about the effects of power, tradition and patriotism. Unlike both *Ivanhoe* and 'The Coronation', George Soane's adaptation pays no compliment to the new monarch, but acts instead as a powerful reminder of all those people (and not simply the Jews) who were excluded from society by the ceremonial extravagances of nationhood.

Notes

1 Richard Ford, *Dramatisations of Scott's Novels: A Catalogue* (Oxford, Oxford Bibliographical Society, Bodleian Library, 1979), pp. 15–27.

2 Henry Adelbert White, *Sir Walter Scott's Novels on the Stage* (New Haven, CT, Yale University Press; Oxford, Oxford University Press, 1927), p. 102.

3 *Ivanhoe; or The Jew's Daughter; A Melo Dramatic Romance, in Three Acts. First Performed at the Surrey Theatre, on Thursday, January 20, 1820*, by Thomas Dibdin (London, Roach, 1820), p. vi.

4 The term comes from a letter to a Miss Smith, who was to act in a production of *The Lady of the Lake*, dated 18 December 1810. See Sir Walter Scott, *The Letters of Sir Walter Scott*, ed. H. J. C. Grierson, (London, Constable, 1935), Vol. V, p. 411.

5 Ford suggests that Scott attended adaptations of *Rob Roy*, *St Ronan's*

Well, The Lady of the Lake, The Heart of Mid-Lothian, George Herriot and *Mary Stuart* as well as the French operatic version of *Ivanhoe*. See Ford, *Dramatisations*, p. vi.

6 Sir Walter Scott, *The Journal of Sir Walter Scott*, ed. W. E. K. Anderson (Oxford, Clarendon Press, 1972), journal entry for Tuesday 31 October 1826, p. 226. See also the brief discussion of this opera and other adaptations of *Ivanhoe* in A. N. Wilson, *The Laird of Abbotsford: A View of Sir Walter Scott* (Oxford, Oxford University Press, 1980), pp. 145–6.

7 Scott, *The Journal*, p. 10.

8 Scott, *The Letters*, Vol. V., pp. 149–50.

9 Sir Walter Scott, 'Introductory Epistle' to *The Fortunes of Nigel. By the Author of 'Waverly, Kenilworth,' &c,* (Edinburgh, Archibald Constable; London, Hurst, Robinson, 1822), pp. xliv–xlv.

10 Chris R. Vanden Bossche, 'Culture and economy in *Ivanhoe*', *Nineteenth-Century Literature*, 42:1 (June 1987) 46–72, p. 46.

11 W. T. Moncrieff, Preface to *Ivanhoe; or, The Jewess* (1820), quoted in White, *Sir Walter Scott's Novels on the Stage*, p. 111.

12 [J. L. Adolphus], *Letters to Richard Heber, Esq. M.P.* (2nd edn, 1822), quoted in John O. Hayden (ed.), *Scott: The Critical Heritage* (London, Routledge, 1970), p. 208.

13 From the information provided by Richard Ford, Pocock was responsible for the following adaptations: *The Antiquary* (1818), *Rob Roy Macgregor; or, Auld Lang Syne!* (1818), *Montrose; or, The Children of the Mist* (1822), *Nigel; or, The Crown Jewels* (1823), *Peveril of the Peak* (1826), *Woodstock* (1826) and *Cavaliers and Roundheads* (1835; an adaptation of *Old Mortality*). See Ford, *Dramatisations*.

14 Ian Duncan, *Modern Romance and Transformations of the Novel: The Gothic, Scott, Dickens* (Cambridge, Cambridge University Press, 1992), p. 5; the passage by Moretti with which Duncan is engaging is taken from *The Way of the World: The Bildungsroman in European Culture* (London, Verso, 1987), p. 251, n. 55.

15 *Quarterly Review*, XXVI (1822), p. 110.

16 Unsigned notice, *Monthly Magazine*, xlix (February 1820) 71, quoted in Hayden (ed.), *Scott*, p. 177.

17 Scott, 'Introductory Epistle', p. xxvi.

18 Scott, 'Introductory Epistle', pp. xxvii–xxviii. For a useful summary of Scott's attitude to the drama, see Margaret Ball, *Sir Walter Scott as a Critic of Literature*, Columbia University Press, 1907; reprinted, Port Washington, NY, Kennikat Press, 1966), especially pp. 46–59.

19 Georg Lukacs, *The Historical Novel*, transl. Hannah and Stanley Mitchel, (London, Merlin Press, 1962), p. 90.

20 Lukacs, *The Historical Novel*, p. 104.
21 Lukacs, *The Historical Novel*, p. 126.
22 Lukacs, *The Historical Novel*, p. 139.
23 *Quarterly Review*, XXVI (1822) 130.
24 Lukacs, *The Historical Novel*, p. 142.
25 Lukacs, *The Historical Novel*, p. 97.
26 Peter Brooks, *The Melodramatic Imagination: Balzac, Henry James, Melodrama, and the Mode of Excess* (New Haven, CT and London, Yale University Press, 1976), p. 17.
27 Otto Ludwig, quoted in Lukacs, *The Historical Novel*, p. 128.
28 Sir Walter Scott, *Ivanhoe*, ed. Ian Duncan (Oxford, Oxford University Press, 1996), p. 45. All references to the novel are to this edition.
29 Simon Shepherd and Peter Womack, *English Drama: A Cultural History* (Oxford, Blackwell, 1996), pp. 198–9.
30 Shepherd and Womack, *English Drama*, p. 203.
31 Shepherd and Womack, *English Drama*, p. 201.
32 *The Hebrew. A Drama, In Five Acts, As Performed At the Theatre-Royal, Drury Lane*, by George Soane (London, John Lowndes, 1820), p. 7.
33 John Sutherland, *The Life of Walter Scott: A Critical Biography*, (Oxford, Blackwell, 1995), p. 228.
34 Sutherland, *The Life of Walter Scott*, p. 229.
35 Sutherland, *The Life of Walter Scott*, pp. 231–2.
36 Michael Ragussis, 'Writing nationalist history: England, the conversion of the Jews, and Ivanhoe', *ELH*, 60 (1993) 181–215, p. 196.
37 Ragussis, 'Writing nationalist history', p. 202
38 Anne Aresty Naman, *The Jew in the Victorian Novel: Some Relationships Between Prejudice and Art* (New York, AMS Press, 1980), p. 20.
39 Ian Duncan, 'Introduction' to Scott, *Ivanhoe*, p. xxv.
40 Scott, *Ivanhoe*, p. xxv, n. 28.
41 Anastasia Nikolopoulou, 'Historical disruptions: the Walter Scott melodramas', in Michael Hays and Anastasia Nikolopoulou (eds), *Melodrama: The Cultural Emergence of a Genre* (New York, St Martin's Press, 1996), p. 137.
42 William Hazlitt, 'The drama: No. IV' from the *London Magazine*, April 1820, in Hazlitt, *The Works of William Hazlitt*, ed. P. P. Hazlitt (London and Toronto, Dent, 1930–34), Vol. 18, p. 314.
43 See, for example, Shepherd and Womack, *English Drama*, p. 194: 'in melodrama the proper purposeful drama was now mixed, inextricably, with the improper 'purposeless' form against which it was always contrasted.'

44 Hazlitt, 'The drama: No. IV' from the *London Magazine*, p. 315.
45 The *London Magazine; and Monthly Critical and Dramatic Review*, I, p. 429; quoted in Ford, *Dramatisations*, p. 21.
46 Sutherland, *The Life of Walter Scott*, p. 229.
47 Marilyn Gaull, *English Romanticism: The Human Context* (New York and London, W. W. Norton, 1988), pp. 86–7.

CHAPTER FOUR

The professional writer: adaptations of Dickens's early novels

As was the case with Sir Walter Scott, the popularity of Charles Dickens's novels resulted in a profusion of stage adaptations, particularly those which originated at the minor, 'illegitimate' theatres of London.[1] Like Scott, Dickens possessed an ambiguous attitude towards dramatists who rewrote his work for the theatre. On the one hand, he would often attend productions and comment favourably upon the acting and the adaptation itself; indeed, at one point he proposed to write his own dramatisation of *Oliver Twist*.[2] On the other hand, he was frequently angered, frustrated or embarrassed by theatrical versions of the novels. In his biography, John Forster records going with Dickens to see what was probably George Almar's *Oliver Twist. A Serio-Comic Burletta* at the Surrey Theatre in the autumn of 1838 and remembers how 'in the middle of the first scene he laid himself down upon the floor in the corner of the box and never rose from it until the drop scene fell'.[3] Dickens's own *Oliver Twist* was, of course, published serially in Bentley's *Miscellany* and the final instalment did not appear until April 1839: what Dickens was witnessing at the Surrey Theatre was one of many adaptations of his novels that came in front of an audience before the original work had been completed by its author. Such dramatic anticipations of the author's conclusions highlight the issues of artistic and commercial autonomy and control that are raised by adaptations during this period. As the role of the writer of imaginative fiction came increasingly to be seen as a professional one in which an author's productions were sold within a literary marketplace, the writer's attempts to maintain the integrity of his or her literary works could be linked to his or her attempts to define and secure their position within the social hierarchy. To have one's work mangled by a hack from one of the minor theatres could have a very adverse effect upon the literary and social aspirations of an ambitious young writer.

Dickens's rise from humble beginnings to a position of public prominence and influence was (if one accepts as a given his enormous talent) achieved entirely through his impressive ability to take control of his own literary career.[4] His achievement can be seen as an ideal fulfilment of the middle-class ambition to prosper through one's own industry and effort, and yet, throughout his writings, one can detect a constant fear of the nightmarish reverse of this ideal in which the rise is replaced by a perilous fall into the lower depths of society from which he had exerted so much effort to differentiate himself. Such a vision is tellingly presented in an early piece of Dickens's journalism, 'Shabby-genteel people', which was originally written for the *Morning Chronicle* in 1834 before being collected in *Sketches By Boz*. In this short essay, Dickens begins by describing a specific example of the kind of person he is writing about:

> We were once haunted by a shabby-genteel man; he was bodily present to our senses all day, and he was in our mind's eye all night. The man of whom Sir Walter Scott speaks in his Demonology, did not suffer half the persecution from his imaginary gentleman usher in black velvet, than we sustained from our friend in quondam black cloth. He first attracted our notice, by sitting opposite to us in the reading room at the British Museum; and what made the man more remarkable was, that he always had before him a couple of shabby-genteel books – two old dog's-eared folios, in mouldy worm-eaten covers, which had once been smart. He was in his chair every morning, just as the clock struck ten; he was always the last to leave the room in the afternoon; and when he did, he quitted it with the air of a man who knew not where else to go for warmth and quiet. There he used to sit all day, as close to the table as possible, in order to conceal the lack of buttons on his coat: with an old hat carefully deposited at his feet, where he evidently flattered himself it escaped observation.[5]

The 'bodily' presence of the shabby-genteel man serves as an index of the fears which 'haunt' the young Dickens as he embarks upon the first stages of his literary career. The writer and this epitome of shabby-gentility sit facing one another, one acting as an effective mirror image of the other. What implicitly unites them is the potential power of the book-as-cultural-icon. The shabby-genteel individual attempts to hide his enforced poverty and lack* of employment behind the appearance of intellectual labour signalled by the constant presence of 'a couple of shabby-genteel books'. The importance of these books is not contained within the fact that they can be read but rather that their presence, within the library, ensures access to an otherwise unobtainable 'warmth and quiet'. Books provide the appearance of social status and thus enable this man to share material benefits which would not normally be available to someone of his social station.

However, it is Dickens's own self-presentation within the context of this scene which is particularly significant for the present discussion. Whilst the reader of the article is aware of Dickens's voice, his own 'bodily' presence within the British Museum, and his activities there, remain somewhat obscured. If the regularity and length of time spent reading (or, pretending to read) by the shabby-genteel man are worthy of note, so too must be the time spent in the reading room by Dickens, who is there to observe the man's arrival and departure every day. The two figures form a pair: the one using reading as a screen to hide his social decline, the other employing reading, literary research and writing as a vehicle for social ascent. Like the shabby-genteel reader, Dickens the writer feels a need to display his own reading in order to achieve effect. The passage proclaims its own literary credentials by citing Scott's *Letters on Demonology and Witchcraft* to provide authority for the young writer's observations. It would be tempting to suggest that it was this very book that Dickens was reading whilst he observed the man opposite him were it not more revealing to note that Scott's book appeared in the first volume of Murray's Home Library Series of 1830. In light of this, Scott's work becomes part of the programme of self-improvement through reading that underpins the present interpretation of Dickens's article. At the end of the piece, Dickens speaks more generally about shabby-genteel men and observes that a 'shabby-genteel man may have no occupation, or he may be a corn-agent, or a coal-agent, or a wine-merchant, or a collector of debts, or a broker's assistant, or a broken down attorney. He may be a clerk of the lowest order, or a contributor to the press of the same grade.'[6] The final sentence introduces a fleetingly personal note: in 1834 Dickens had only just commenced work as a full-time journalist, having previously been employed as a clerk in a solicitor's office. As clerk and now journalist, Dickens is very much aware of the lack of financial and material security belonging to a person of his social class. In order to succeed in his ambitions he would have to deploy his reading and writing to full effect and, furthermore, be in a position to control that effect amongst the reading public. As will be seen, the existence of numerous adaptations of his work complicated such control.

However, although Dickens was an astute manager of his literary affairs, it is important to register the role played by chance and apparent accident in the unfolding of his literary career. What we now think of as the first of Dickens's novels, the *Pickwick Papers*, was, as is well known, brought into being when the publishers Chapman and Hall approached the writer (who was not their first choice) to contribute a written text to accompany sporting plates produced by the illustrator Robert Seymour.[7] Dickens, then, was not commissioned to write a novel nor perhaps did he intend the monthly instalments to conform to that genre when he commenced writing. Having said this, Kathryn Chittick has persuasively suggested that, by the end of the serialisation, Dickens had come to see *Pickwick Papers* as the starting point for a successful career as a serious literary novelist.[8] If this is the case, it became even more important for him to distinguish his literary productions from less serious, ephemeral publications of the kind that he was originally asked to write for Chapman and Hall and from the equally ephemeral and yet more populist adaptations of his novels in the minor theatres. One text which can be seen to epitomise all the qualities which Dickens was striving to differentiate his own work from was Pierce Egan's *Life in London; or, the Day and Night Scenes of Jerry Hawthorne, Esq., and his Elegant Friend Corinthian Tom, Accompanied by Bob Logic, the Oxonian, in their Rambles and Sprees Through the Metropolis*, which came out in monthly instalments from October 1820 to July 1821 and which, as many critics have observed, formed an undeniable model for at least the initial instalments of *Pickwick Papers*.[9] Each number of *Life in London* contained illustrations by either George or Robert Cruikshank which provided the focus for the accompanying prose descriptions by Egan. As a result, and as the full title suggests, the narrative is discontinuous and rambling, following the escapades of the protagonists through high and, particularly notoriously, low London life. The dialogue is liberally peppered with low-life cant and slang which gives the prose a highly distinctive and yet, at the same time, appealingly disreputable quality. Throughout the 1820s, *Life in London* was enormously popular and this popularity resulted in numerous instances of plagiarism and adaptation. When Dickens's *Pickwick Papers* later achieved even greater popularity in what appeared to be a very similar format, inevitable comparisons were made. This was particularly the case when adaptations were advertised: the playbill for an 1837 production, for example, begins by proclaiming that 'Every age hath its "form and pressure;" and since the days of TOM AND JERRY, nothing has appeared in the vast field of literature like the PICKWICK CLUB'.[10] *Life in London* was decidedly not a serious literary publication and such comparisons would hinder Dickens's career as a writer of serious novels. Consequently, Dickens attempted to deny links between himself and Egan, as can be seen, for example, in a generally favourable letter (from November 1838) which discusses the merits of an adaptation of *Nicholas Nickleby* by Edward Stirling:

> My general objection to the adaptation of any unfinished work of mine simply is, that being badly done and worse acted it tends to vulgarize the characters, to destroy or weaken in the minds of those who see them the impressions I have endeavoured to create, and consequently lessen the after-interest in their progress. No such objection can exist for a moment where the thing is so admirably done in every respect as you have done it in this instance …
>
> Would you think me very unreasonable if I asked you not to compare Nicholas with Tom and Jerry?[11]

Dickens offers an argument about adaptations of his work which balances artistic considerations concerning the effects he has 'endeavoured to create' with a commercial sense that, if an audience has seen a (less satisfactory) 'conclusion' to the story, they will have less 'after-interest' in the 'progress' of the characters. Yet, in addition to this, there is a fear of the potential of these adaptations to 'vulgarize' his novels in such a way as to make possible genuine comparisons with Egan's *Life in London* or stage adaptations of it.

The letter is worth quoting at some length because it presents a more moderate attitude towards adaptation than that with which most readers will be familiar from the satirical portrait of the adapting playwright as the 'literary gentleman' in Chapter 48 of *Nicholas Nickleby*. In that instance, however, it is significant that the object of Dickens's satire is a specific playwright, namely William Thomas Moncrieff, whose adaptation of *Nicholas Nickleby* appeared at the Strand Theatre on 29 May 1839 (six months after Stirling's play opened at the Adelphi).[12] Moncrieff was already known to Dickens because of a particularly acrimonious dispute over an earlier adaptation of *Pickwick Papers*, but, perhaps of equal importance, his name would be extremely familiar as the most famous adapter of Egan's *Life in London* as *Tom and Jerry; or, Life in London: An Operatic Extravaganza* (1821). In the play-bills and the published texts of his adaptations of Dickens, Moncrieff was frequently styled as 'the author of Tom and Jerry'. Here, then, was a playwright who threatened to foreground the most 'vulgar' aspects of Dickens's work and reassociate him with those very areas of literary production from which he hoped to disassociate himself. Indeed, further examination of Moncrieff's life and work reveals him to be a touchstone for Dickens's fears concerning his early career as a professional novelist. Moncrieff emerges, as will be seen, as a product of the same unsettling cultural and commercial forces which determined the nature of Dickens's success as a professional writer.[13] The next section of the present chapter focuses on points of similarity and difference between Moncrieff and Dickens as they are foregrounded by their disagreements over the practice of adaptation.

GIVEN DICKENS'S DESIRE TO distance his work from that of Moncrieff, it is important to register from the outset the similarity of their social backgrounds. Moncrieff was born in 1794 as the son of a London tradesman and, at an early age, he, like Dickens, became a clerk in a solicitor's office before leaving to make a living by his writing. The crucial difference between the two writers lies perhaps in their ultimate choice of literary profession, and it is a difference which reflects the changing status of the novelist and the dramatist in the early decades of the nineteenth century. Whilst Dickens might look upon Moncrieff as a derivative hack without artistic merit or purpose, it is clear from Moncrieff's own writings that he too possessed a sense of literary ambition – although all too often he felt this to be compromised by the material conditions within which he, as a playwright, was forced to work. Giving evidence before the Parliamentary Select Committee on Dramatic Literature in 1832, Moncrieff bemoaned the parlous state of the playwright's profession:

> As the drama is at present constituted, it is impossible for any man, whose misfortunes may oblige him to resort to that species of writing, to obtain a fair remuneration for his labour and talent; the laxity that has crept into the different theatres in London renders it impossible, except by mere accident. A man may write a good piece and get well paid for it, but he must wait a long time.[14]

Unlike Dickens, whose popularity and success with serial publication would ensure him vast financial rewards, Moncrieff presents a picture of the dramatist as one who is incapable of prospering through his writing. He attacks the 'major part' of theatre managers as simply 'money-making men' devoid of artistic interest or talent and attacks the predominance of 'all that melodramatic nonsense which we see' in the contemporary minor theatres where he was largely forced to make his living.

Of course, Moncrieff himself was responsible for much of the 'melodramatic nonsense' that made its way into the theatre, but he is none the less a man who is genuinely troubled by the quality of the plays he is required to produce. In other aspects of his writing, particularly his poetry, he reveals a perhaps greater degree of literary seriousness. In 1829 he privately published a collection of poems which, the Preface claims, had been written to please his new wife who had unfortunately died before the project could be brought to completion. The volume is introduced with quotations from Petrarch and Ninernois and the poet declares in the Preface that many of the poems 'are merely imitations of various passages that afforded me pleasure during the progress of a very desultory course of reading'. He adds that he has 'found amusement in noting down the various coincidences with my Poems, which I have discovered in other writers, and in pointing out to whom I have been indebted for my ideas'.[15] This, then, is a very 'literary' volume and, despite the apparent disclaimer present in his use of the word 'desultory', Moncrieff is clearly keen to demonstrate his poetic reading as an index of his qualification for the role of 'poet'. In a later letter, written in 1840, requesting financial support from the Royal Literary Fund, Moncrieff describes how this 'Volume of Poems' which dates from 'better times, when I had a private press of my own' was published 'to show that I had a taste for more elegant pursuits of literature, though interest compelled me to exercise what little talent I possessed in other channels'.[16] Elsewhere, his poetry is not quite so polished, but it does exhibit a satirical purpose which invests it with a different kind of seriousness. In *The March of Intellect, A Comic Poem* (1830), for example, Moncrieff touches upon similar concerns to those of Dickens in *Oliver Twist*. He describes (in, admittedly, comic fashion) the effects of education amongst the lower classes and, particularly, in the workhouse:

> LVIII.
> Words now grow high – reform! reform!
>   All's uproar and disquiet;
> The beadle hears the rising storm,
>   And comes to quell the riot.
>
> LIX.
> True member he of the elect,
>   He speaks like a recorder;
> Begs they will church and state respect,
>   And keep the social order.
>
> LX.
> The vestry will the poor maintain,
>   That they may not grow thinner;
> Their state they will discuss again,
>   And meet and have a dinner.
>
> LXI.
> The vestry meet – a rate is made
>   To pay the current quarter;
> The March of Intellect's displayed
>   In champagne and rose water.[17]

Such examples might not reveal Moncrieff to be a great poet but they do suggest that his motivations were not merely financial and that he had literary goals that took him beyond the simple aspirations of the hack writer.

When it came to adaptation, however, Moncrieff clearly had difficulty balancing artistic autonomy on the one hand (both his own and that of the author whose work he was adapting) and the demands of the literary and theatrical market on the other. In the last chapter reference was made to the 'Advertisement' to his adaptation of Scott's *Ivanhoe* as *Ivanhoe! or, The Jewess. A Chivalric Play* (1820). It is worth quoting here in full to reveal the strange rhetorical contortions into which Moncrieff's divided opinions lead him:

> I have prefixed my name to this Drama, as having *written* it, in imitation of many contemporary Playwrights, who have lately obtained the reputation of excellent Dramatists, on no better grounds than paste, shears, and a Scottish Novel. But it will very soon be discovered, that I have scarcely written fifty lines of it; and, could I have performed my task without even that addition, I would willingly have done so; conscious, the less we modern dramatists mix up our own with the works of an author like the great UNKNOWN, the better it must ultimately turn out for all parties. I have a strong suspicion that my Drama will prove the best that may appear on the subject, from the circumstance of its containing less *original* matter than any other, and the very few *improvements* I have attempted on my text. I *wrote* my Drama as soon as the Romance of "Ivanhoe" was published, in the hope of being first in the market with so saleable commodity, but was much surprised to find *other* WRITERS were *three* weeks before me, they having obtained their materiel [*sic*], *par grace* three weeks previous to publication. I have therefore to request, that the Author of the Romance of "Ivanhoe", in consideration of the tenderness I have shown in mangling his Work, will do me the favour in future to let me have the proof sheets of his productions the moment he receives them from the printer.[18]

The tone of this passage is extremely difficult to judge, shifting as it does from apparent humility to evident self-assertion (if not outright arrogance). Moncrieff begins by almost denying his right to claim for himself the status of author for a work which, as he admits, is still more properly Scott's than his own (although his contribution to the play is far more than the 'fifty lines' he mentions). This seeming humility extends beyond Moncrieff as an individual to the position of 'contemporary Playwrights' in general and appears to suggest that, as a class, 'modern dramatists' should not aspire to reach the same artistic achievements as those represented by Scott's novels. Within this class of dramatists, however, Moncrieff soon asserts his priority as having written the 'best' adaptation of the novel and then proceeds to observe, audaciously within the context of the argument so far, how he has made a few 'improvements' to Scott's original. This audacity is extended by his parting request to be supplied with the proofs of any future Scott novels so that he can be ahead of the market with 'so saleable a commodity'. Is this a serious request? Or is it an ironic joke which reveals a cynical awareness of the commodification of culture he is participating in? Does his reference to the 'tender' mangling of *Ivanhoe* represent a genuine recognition of poor artistry or an ironic anticipation of the criticism which will be levelled against his dramatisation by the more 'serious' of Scott's advocates? It would seem that the passage refuses to answer these questions, but this very resistance can be interpreted as a sign of the difficult negotiations taking place between concepts of 'originality', the status of the author (and, particularly, the changing relationship between novelist and dramatist), and the role of the marketplace in matters of literary production.

All of these issues were brought sharply to the fore in the often acrimonious disputes caused by Moncrieff's adaptations of *Pickwick Papers* and *Nicholas Nickleby*. As is suggested by the work of Kathryn Chittick, the context for such disagreements is to be found in Dickens's changing conception of himself as a writer and the work of his supporters who promoted his work through prominent and influential reviews. The most important of these reviewers was John Forster who, from the very beginning, championed Dickens's claims to be considered as a major novelist. In an *Examiner* review of the final instalments of *Pickwick Papers*, Forster is already asserting the canonical status of the young writer's work:

> it is more than likely that not a few generations of people will have their fortunes and adventures in the real world and die and be forgotten with them, while the familiar people of this pleasant book shall still remain as they are now, unchanging and unchangeable, and hearty and pleasant as ever. The established English novelists may without much scruple, we

think, open their arms to receive another set of deathless folks into their old and genial family.[19]

After the publication of just one book, Forster is ready to grant Dickens and his characters literary immortality. The novel (if such it is) becomes disassociated from the material exigencies of the 'real' world and exists instead in a state of quasi-heavenly elevation where it remains 'unchanging and unchangeable'. By interpreting Dickens's fiction in this way, Forster renders himself particularly resistant to the notion of theatrical adaptations of the novels which, by definition, must change that which he insists is unchangeable.

That this was the case is evident from the hostility with which he greeted Moncrieff's *Sam Weller, or, the Pickwickians* when it was performed at the New Strand Theatre in July 1837. Although he offers fulsome praise for many of the performances (particularly Hammond's portrayal of Weller), Forster clearly disapproves of adaptations of Dickens's work and particularly adaptations by writers such as Moncrieff. At first he simply seems to be criticising those aspects of the play which originate from the dramatist rather than the novelist. He notes (perhaps ironically) the apologetic tone of Moncrieff's comments in the playbills and proceeds to observe that it 'would have been well if Mr Moncrieff had acted a little more with the spirit he professes, and if, when the insertion of his own sheer nonsense and vulgarity could serve no dramatic purpose, he had been content to let the characters say something a little more resembling in wit and humour what had been set down for them by their successful originator'.[20] The model of adaptation implied here is one which changes its original as little as possible, treating the novel as an embryonic script which can be translated almost directly on to the stage. It is a model which recalls Moncrieff's own account of his practice in his adaptation of *Ivanhoe*, but it is also one which ironically foregrounds any (inevitable) departures from the original text. Forster's criticism of these aspects of the play is particularly harsh, but it should be noted that, yet again, what is highlighted is the element of 'vulgarity' which Moncrieff's version allegedly brings to Dickens's novel. As the review continues, it becomes clear that such vulgarity is being employed rhetorically to differentiate the work of Dickens from that of hack writing of a lower, more populist order. The adaptation, Forster opines, reveals 'a total absence of perception, both on the part of dramatist and actors, of that delicate satire and deep meaning – often hid beneath the surface – in which the author of the *Pickwick Papers*, in common with all the great comic writers, is so eminently and peculiarly happy'. The 'delicacy' of Dickens's novel is thus contrasted with the 'vulgarity' of its adaptation. Moreover, the review as a whole suggests that the 'deep meaning' of the novel can never be recreated by the essentially superficial medium of theatrical representation, particularly by the scant talent of a 'third-rate actor' or 'the boisterous pantomime of the half-dozen miserable supernumeraries of a minor theatre'. The criticism therefore implicitly makes a distinction between the potentially 'high' art of the novel and the usually 'low' art of the popular theatre and this distinction extends to a differentiation between the corresponding powers of aesthetic discrimination to be found in novel readers and theatregoers. Whereas it is implied that competent readers possess a sufficiently refined sensibility to be able to probe the text for a 'hidden meaning' which resides 'far below the surface', the audience at the New Strand Theatre in 1837 seemed completely oblivious to the finer points of criticism put forward in the *Examiner*. 'As it is,' writes Forster, 'the house has been crowded every night, and the audience have expressed "unequivocal satisfaction," notwithstanding that the burletta is some half-hour longer than a five-act tragedy, and in spite of the execrable acting of Mr J. Lee.'

Moncrieff was, perhaps understandably, enraged by this review and, in a long 'Advertisement' to the published version of *Sam Weller*, he replied to it in terms which suggest an acute understanding of the issues which underpin Forster's arguments. Despite the anger and sense of personal insult, therefore, Moncrieff's response displays a broader perspective of the literary and cultural consequences of the quarrel. His opening gambit is again to adopt a tone of apparent humility before the 'very original, graphic, and clever' achievement of Dickens in the *Pickwick Papers* but, as he proceeds, one begins to detect a pride in his own contribution to the adaptation:

> The Papers had been pronounced to be wholly undramatic; – two very talented gentlemen, to use a newspaper term, had both attempted the task, and failed – the one, from sticking too closely to his original – the

other, through departing too widely from it. It struck me, they were to be *made* dramatic. I knew well their author had never contemplated the production of them in a dramatic shape, or he would have formed a regular plot, and given a continuity to the work, which alone is wanting, to rank it with the finest comic fictions of any age or country.[21]

Moncrieff first makes an argument for the talent that is required (and in particular, his own talent) to adapt a novel for the stage. The success of such plays, he argues in opposition to Forster, is dependent upon a necessary departure from the original novel and an awareness of specifically dramatic requirements. Second, he implicitly disagrees with Forster's evaluation of Dickens's achievement as a novelist. Whilst there is what appears to be genuine admiration for the quality of Dickens as a writer (and this is something from which Moncrieff never seems to depart), he suggests that there are grounds for denying *Pickwick Papers* the high literary status claimed for it by Forster because of its lack of a 'regular plot'. As Moncrieff must be aware, this lack is a result of the generic expectations Dickens was working within when he commenced the project. Rather than portraying *Pickwick Papers* as an embryonic canonical novel, Moncrieff provides a subtle reminder of its generic affinities with more popular (and populist) productions such as *Life in London* (with which, of course, his own name was inevitably associated).

What Moncrieff seems in particular to be objecting to, however, is what he perceives to be Forster's critical project to create rigid categories of 'high' and 'low' art. His strategy is to defend Dickens from the appropriation of his work by what he terms the 'high intellectual' critics:

Mr Dickens has, by far, too much genius, to nourish any of the petty feelings evinced by his Fostering friends! whose articles, being those of the 'High Intellectual' Sunday-school of criticism, are greatly too genteel and abstruse, for every day reading, but must be kept for Lord's day examination only! Why these gentry should object to my having dramatised Mr Dickens, I cannot conceive. Sir WALTER SCOTT – a name, I humbly submit, of sufficient merit, to be mentioned in the same page with the writer of the 'Pickwick Club,' always looked upon Mr Pocock's and Mr Terry's stage versions of those immortal fictions, 'Rob Roy' and 'Ivanhoe' rather as a compliment than otherwise, and I had undoubted precedent, for what I did, in the instance of the first dramatic writer of all time – SHAKESPEARE! who has scarcely a play, that is not founded on some previous drama, history, chronicle, popular tale, or story. What then means the twaddle of these 'high intellectuals', in so pathetically condoling with Mr Dickens, on the penalties he pays for his popularity, in being put on the stage? Let these 'high intellectuals' speak to Mr Dickens's publishers, and they will learn, it has rendered them, by increasing the sale, the most fortunate Chapmen and dealers![22]

As with so many of Moncrieff's outbursts the argument might be slightly confused, but the confusion itself is revealing. Drawing upon the precedent of Scott, he wants to present an adaptation as a 'compliment' to a writer of great stature. Whilst *Rob Roy* and *Ivanhoe* might be 'immortal fictions' (in much the same way as, according to Forster, *Pickwick Papers*), the existence of adaptations only highlights their status and underlines both their popularity and enduring quality. At the same time, in what Dickens was to see as an audacious move, Moncrieff makes what could seem like a rather elevated claim for himself by citing Shakespeare as the primary exponent of the adapter's art. On the one hand the playwright is seen as having a secondary status to the original novelist, on the other he is capable of surpassing the narrative's originator and achieving a significant work in his own right. Whilst he does this, Moncrieff also grounds Dickens's novel in the 'real' world from which Forster's 'high intellectual' criticism had attempted to remove it, by reminding his reader of the economic conditions of the literary marketplace.

The general thrust of Moncrieff's argument would seem to be that Shakespeare, Scott, Dickens, Pocock, Terry and himself are all professional writers worthy of serious attention who write to earn a living and are dependent upon the popularity of their works to be successful. He is clearly not saying that some works cannot be better than others, but he is saying that all kinds and genres of literary production are worthy of equal attention. This he sees as being denied by the tone and content of Forster's criticism which, for Moncrieff, adopts an 'abstruse' and yet simultaneously prescriptive terminology in order to achieve its ends:

the public will soon begin to feel with me their gorge rise, at any article in which such phrases, as 'fine spirit of individuality,' 'keen relish of all the more refined impulses of our nature' – 'exquisite sense of humanity,'

&c.&c. appear; they will exclaim, oh! this is one of the 'high intellectual Sunday-school of criticism articles,' and reserve it till they wish to read off to sleep.[23]

Having been accused of 'vulgarity', Moncrieff responds with an accusation of elitism and pretentiousness. What is clearly emerging here is a recognisable polarisation between 'high' and 'low' literature. However, it is equally important to observe that Moncrieff's accusation is directed not at the novel itself but at the criticism which attempts to interpret it according to certain social and aesthetic criteria.

Dickens's response to Moncrieff's 'Advertisement', contained in a letter to Forster, translates the 'vulgarity' of the adaptation itself into a charge of personal vulgarity and disreputableness:

> I recollect this 'member of the dramatic-authors's society' bringing an action once against Chapman, who rented the City Theatre ... The defendant's plea was that the plaintiff was always drunk, and had not fulfilled his contract. Well; if the *Pickwick* has been the means of putting a few shillings in the vermin-eaten pockets of so miserable a creature, and has saved him from a workhouse or a jail, let him empty out his little pot of filth and welcome. I am quite content to have been the means of relieving him.[24]

The dismissive, and yet evidently angry, contempt displayed here indicates that Moncrieff's 'Advertisement' had struck a nerve: unable to undo the fact of *Sam Weller* or its popularity, Dickens constructs Moncrieff as a miserable (and somewhat disreputable and morally bankrupt) beggar who is worthy of begrudging charity. Forster, who relays the contents of this letter in his *Life*, makes no reference to his own part in provoking Moncrieff's comments, but he too was angered by the playwright's observations. Like Dickens, he responded by descending to the level of personal abuse, but he did so in a more public fashion. In a short *Examiner* review (which is favourable within the limits allowed by his views on the desirability of any form of adaptation) of another dramatisation of *Pickwick Papers* by Charles Selby, Forster takes the opportunity of making a telling but indirect personal attack on the author of *Sam Weller*. Selby's play is described as possibly 'the best attempt' so far:

and certainly infinitely superior to what we may designate as the *Wine Vault School* of dramatic authorship. It is due to Mr. Selby, whom we believe to be a respectable, well-conducted person, to say thus much; but at the same time we are bound to add in charity that we see no objection to any worn-out dramatic hack earning a few honest pounds from the vulgar mutilation of this or any other work if he can get his piece accepted.[25]

Forster evidently takes his cue from Dickens: Moncrieff is presented as a drunken, dissolute and talentless hack who is contrasted with Charles Selby who is 'respectable' and 'well-conducted' – and who also knows his place. What is clearly taking place in both Dickens's letter and this review is that the perceived 'vulgarity' of the adaptation is being explained away by mapping the vulgarity on to the private characteristics of the individual playwright. Neither Dickens nor Forster respond to the issues raised by Moncrieff's arguments: instead they reconstruct him as a character who is not worthy of a response.

This reconstruction of Moncrieff was carried to what could be seen as its logical conclusion when Dickens introduced a satirical portrait of him into Chapter 48 of *Nicholas Nickleby*. The immediate occasion for this was the appearance of Moncrieff's adaptation of Dickens's novel as *Nicholas Nickleby and Poor Smike; or, The Victim of the Yorkshire School*, first performed on 20 May 1839 at the New Strand Theatre. At the benefit party for Mr Crummles, Nicholas meets a 'literary gentleman' who 'had dramatised in his time two hundred and forty-seven novels as fast as they had come out – and some of them faster than they had come out – and *was* a literary gentleman in consequence'.[26] The repeated and increasingly ironic use of the terms 'literary' and 'gentleman' continues the terms of the ongoing argument between Moncrieff on the one hand and Forster and Dickens on the other, and it also underlines the contested and interrelated nature of both categories. Dickens hoped to become a 'gentleman' through serious 'literary' endeavour, but, in order to do so, he had to define himself against the debased forms of popular entertainment that were epitomised for him in the person of Moncrieff. The literary highground has to be regained (or, rather, distinguished from) that inhabited by the hack writers of the minor theatres. Dickens begins by retrieving

Shakespeare (whom the 'literary gentleman', with 'vulgar' familiarity, insists upon calling 'Bill') from Moncrieff's grasp. Nicholas admits that Shakespeare dramatised stories which 'had previously appeared in print' but emphasises that there is a vast difference between this and the activities of the contemporary adapter:

> whereas he brought within the magic circle of his genius, traditions peculiarly adapted for his purpose, and turned familiar things into constellations which should enlighten the world for ages, you drag within the magic circle of your dullness, subjects not at all adapted to the purposes of the stage, and debase as he exalted. For instance, you take the uncompleted books of living authors, fresh from their hands, wet from the press, cut, hack, and carve them to the powers and capacities of your actors, and the capability of your theatres, finish unfinished works, hastily and crudely vamp up ideas not yet worked out by their original projector, but which have doubtless cost him many thoughtful days and sleepless nights [...] and then, to crown the whole proceeding, publish in some mean pamphlet, an unmeaning farrago of garbled extracts from his work, to which you put your name as author, with the honourable distinction annexed, of having perpetrated a hundred other outrages of the same description. Now, show me the distinction between such pilfering as this, and picking a man's pocket in the street ...[27]

Moncrieff is presented as no better than a common thief, a talentless hack who mutilates the works of others and claims respect for achievements that he has failed to earn. The passage disrupts the narrative of the novel and gives the impression of a direct and angry attack by Dickens upon Moncrieff. However, such narrative disruption has the ironic effect of reminding the reader of the episodic, relativistic nature of *Nicholas Nickleby* as it was published in monthly instalments. Against Forster's model of a canonical work peopled with 'unchanging and unchangeable' characters, the reader is presented with a text which is evidently grounded in the 'real' world of everyday lived experience; the 'literary gentleman', no matter how fictionalised, is easily identified as a specific, living individual and the author himself is revealed as a victim of personal animosities on the one hand and the vicissitudes of the literary marketplace on the other. No matter how hard Dickens attempts to distinguish himself from Moncrieff, the engagement with him in the pages of *Nicholas Nickleby* acts as a reminder that, at this point in history, both inhabit the same cultural milieu. Nicholas/Dickens conclude their attack on Moncrieff with a personal insult which also revisits the notion of literary immortality: 'I have nothing more to say, than, that if I were a writer of books, and you a thirsty dramatist, I would rather pay your tavern score for six months – large as it might be – than have a niche in the Temple of Fame with you for the humblest corner of my pedestal, through six hundred generations.'[28] Continuing the motif of Moncrieff as a dissolute drunkard, the implication is that his place is in the tavern rather than the 'Temple of Fame'.

Up until this point in the dispute, Moncrieff had invariably seen Dickens as first and foremost a fellow writer who, as such, deserved credit for his talent. Any direct attack was levelled at Forster whom he felt was appropriating Dickens for his own purposes (there is, of course, an irony here) and also being personally abusive towards himself. The satirical portrait in *Nicholas Nickleby* seemingly came as something of a surprise. In a published reply, addressed 'To the Public', Moncrieff begins by stating that 'some of the newspapers having named me as the person intended to be represented by an intemperate and vulgar caricature in the last published number of NICHOLAS NICKLEBY, which without such information I should certainly never have suspected, it may perhaps be necessary to say a few words to set the public right upon the matter'.[29] Moncrieff is perhaps being somewhat disingenuous here, but it is none the less interesting how Dickens has now, by implication, become the 'intemperate and vulgar' writer by descending to such satirical means. Moncrieff elaborates upon this later on in his response:

> With all possible good feeling, I would beg to hint to Mr. Dickens that depreciating the talents of another is but a shallow and envious way of attempting to raise one's own that the calling the offending party a thief, sneering at his pecuniary circumstances, and indulging in empty boasts of tavern treats, are weapons of offence usually resorted to by only the very lowest orders. Nothing is more easy than to be ill-natured. I confess I write for my living, and it is no discredit to Mr. Dickens to say that those who know him best are aware he is as much indebted to his pen for the dinner of the day, as I can possibly be. With respect to the '*six hundred generations*' through which Mr. Dickens expects his 'pedestal should remain in the Temple of Fame,' I can assure him that I have never

anticipated that any credit I might have derived from dramatising 'Nicholas Nickleby' would more than endure beyond as many days.[30]

The tone here seems eminently reasonable and candid: both Dickens and Moncrieff are presented as writers who write for a living and can therefore be seen as in some sense 'professional'. As such, Moncrieff implies, they should treat one another with mutual respect; indeed, they should treat one another as 'gentlemen'. Moncrieff is evidently just as concerned as Dickens not to be associated with what he terms 'the very lowest orders' of society. For Moncrieff, questions of literary immortality are independent of such professional equality: Dickens might be more talented, more popular, and therefore more financially successful, but this should not hide the equivalence of their occupations. For Dickens to admit such an equivalence, however, would be for him to deny the social elevation he aspired to in becoming a 'serious' writer. With their shared social backgrounds, Moncrieff appears like another version of the 'shabby-genteel man' in the *Morning Chronicle* essay. He is a disturbing mirror image representing what Dickens could be: a moderately successful hack writer who is constantly at the mercy of exploitative stage managers and the fickle tastes of audiences within the theatre. In the 'real' world Dickens had to deal with similar problems, but it was necessary for them to be disguised in order for him to achieve a successful self-presentation as a serious novelist, and as a true 'literary gentleman'.

WHATEVER DICKENS'S ATTITUDE to the adaptations that continued to be produced throughout his lifetime, it cannot be denied that they made an enormous contribution to his fame and currency as a writer. An anonymous reviewer in *Fraser's Magazine* for April 1840, for example, notes of *Nicholas Nickleby* that there 'is no need of our going through any of the details of a story so familiarly known to all readers of novels and frequenters of theatres'.[31] The curious element here is that most adaptations of *Nicholas Nickleby*, and particularly those which appeared before the serialisation had been completed, did not tell the same 'story' as Dickens's novel: the order of events was changed and manipulated for theatrical effect, episodes were inserted and omitted, and the denouement anticipated in ways which provided quite different resolutions to the narrative. And yet the reviewer is probably right to suggest that even those people who had not read the novel felt that in some way they already 'knew' it. In the eyes of many people, the characters from the novel had, through adaptation in particular, gained a life outside and independent of the text from which they originated. Some contemporary critics interpreted this as a sign of Dickens's stature as a great imaginative artist. Thus, for example, an anonymous reviewer of *Oliver Twist* in the *Literary Gazette* of 24 November 1838, draws attention to

> one quality which Mr. Dickens has displayed to an extent altogether unequalled, if we except, perhaps, the mighty names of Shakespeare and Scott. We allude to the creation of individual character: to the raising up and embodying of a number of original human beings in so substantial a form, and endowed with such living feelings and passions, and acting in so real and natural a manner, that they immediately become visually, personally, and intimately known to us; and we no more doubt of their existence than if we had seen them in the flesh, conversed with them, and observed their conduct. This was made curiously manifest on the appearance of the characters at the Adelphi and Surrey theatres. All classes instantly recognised them; and boxes, pit, and gallery, exclaimed 'That's such a one, and that's such another,' through the whole of the *dramatis personae* of *Oliver Twist* and *Nicholas Nickleby*. This is true fame.[32]

In many ways this critic follows the lead offered by Forster in that Dickens, at an early stage in his career, is elevated to a quasi-canonical status and is spoken of in the same breath as Scott and Shakespeare. As in Forster's argument, it is Dickens's ability to create apparently 'real' characters that becomes the hallmark of his imaginative genius and yet, in a move which distinguishes his critical strategy from that adopted by Forster, the present reviewer includes within the scope of Dickens's creative influence the 'appearance' (note how the word seems to apply an existence independent of the novels themselves) of the characters in stage adaptations. Whereas Forster describes the characterisation as inherently textual, belonging to a refined reading experience, the reviewer of *Oliver Twist* maintains that the transformation of character through adaptation merely serves to extend and legitimate his claims for Dickens's power as a novelist.

Not all critics responded so favourably to – or put so favourable a gloss upon – the presence of numerous adaptations of stage novels. A particularly interesting critical note is sounded by a somewhat later review of the 'Writings of Charles Dickens' from the *North British Review* of May 1845 in which the reviewer notes that

> In estimating the probable effects of these writings of Mr. Dickens, we must remember that, in the shape of plays, they have been represented at most of the theatres in the country. In this process of transmutation the better and more sober parts necessarily disappear, and the striking figures, amusing low life, smart vulgar conversation, and broad farce, are naturally preserved with care.[33]

This is seemingly more in line with the ideas of Forster and (probably) Dickens himself. The 'transmutation' described turns a novel with serious, moral aspirations into an entertainment which more nearly resembles the representation of 'amusing low life' and 'smart vulgar conversation' more readily associated with Egan's *Life in London* or Moncrieff's adaptation of it as *Tom and Jerry*. Where the reviewer differs from Forster, however, is in his belief that the germs for such immorality are to be found within the novels themselves and that it is in his approach to characterisation that Dickens is largely at fault. In an earlier passage from the same article, the reviewer complains that

> Mr. Dickens never trusts to a vigorous sketch, or a few characteristic touches; he accomplishes his purpose by minute description and copious dialogue, and leaves no work for the imagination of the reader. This leads us to observe, that the vast popularity of these works may, perhaps, in some degree be owing to the indolence of the reading public, and that the very clever 'illustrations' which accompany them all, may have contributed greatly to their success. No reader need ever task his mind's eye to form a picture corresponding to the full description; he has but to turn the page, and there stands the Pickwick, Pecksniff, or Tom Pinch, embodied to his hand, and kindly saving him the labour of thought.[34]

Whilst the specific argument here (that Dickens provides too much detail) might not be the most obvious one, in its broad outlines the passage rehearses what has become a common criticism of 'low' or 'popular' culture: it does not make its reader actively think and therefore contributes to a decline in the nation's mental and moral life. The reviewer begins by associating this tendency within Dickens's work with the written text itself, but then proceeds to focus on the 'very clever' illustrations. There is a reversal here of what one might term Forster's 'depth' model of hidden meaning. The passage suggests that Dickens hides nothing, that he is, in fact, all 'surface' and that the logical extension of this is the presence of visual illustrations which consolidate the impression that what is being called upon is the 'eye' of the 'body' rather than that of the 'mind'.[35] Whether it is intended or not, such criticism evokes the ghost, yet again, of publications such as Egan's *Life in London* which, as has been noted, explicitly gave precedence to the visual over the verbal text: Egan's narrative was structured by the accompanying engravings and this, it will be remembered, was also the intention of Seymour when he originally presented his plans to Chapman and Hall for what was to become the *Pickwick Papers*.

In addition, the *North British Review* article's emphasis upon a translation of written word into visual image evokes the similar processes at work during the production of a stage adaptation.[36] Indeed, the instant recognition of characters on stage from *Oliver Twist* and *Nicholas Nickleby* celebrated by the reviewer in the *Literary Gazette* was probably largely a result of the audience's familiarity with the prior visualisations of them in the illustrations. The likelihood of this being the case is increased when one considers the close relationship that existed between the illustrations and the theatrical productions. From the very beginning, but particularly in versions of the two novels cited by the reviewer, adaptations of Dickens frequently contained a number of 'tableaux' in which illustrations by Phiz or Cruikshank were recreated on the stage. As H. Philip Bolton observes, this 'convention' can be traced back to earlier adaptations of (again) Egan's *Life in London*.[37] What Bolton does not note, however, is that when Moncrieff came to write the most famous version of this book, he saw it primarily as a dramatisation of the visual rather than the verbal text. As he writes in his 'Remarks to the Second Edition' of *Tom and Jerry*: 'But to return to TOM and JERRY, – it need scarcely be stated that it is founded on Cruikshank's inimitable plates of LIFE in LONDON.'[38] In a sense, Moncrieff approaches *Life in London* as Egan's equal; both writers employ their differing literary talents to 'illustrate' the plates provided by the engraver. Although Moncrieff, as has been seen, always thought of his adaptations of Dickens as being versions of the written text, the centrality of the 'illustration-tableau' in the adaptations of this period clearly indicates the importance the playwrights gave to the visual elements of the original volumes which, according to the *North British Review*, contributed to the 'indolence of the reading public'.

At one level, the use of the 'illustration-tableau' depends upon a fairly sophisticated audience appreciation of plates they recognise from the original book. Just as the repetition of large amounts of dialogue from the novels causes the spectator to remember the original reading experience, so the performance of the illustrations calls upon him or her to remember the material presence of the book. At the same time, however, this is also an act of misremembering in that, very often, the tableaux are used to 'illustrate' a quite different narrative moment. Thus, for example, Act III, Scene iii of Edward Stirling's *The Pickwick Club: or, The Age We live In!* (which was first produced at the City of London Theatre on 27 April 1837) takes place in a double-bedded room at the White Horse, Ipswich. Pickwick enters the room, hears someone else and hides in the four-poster bed. Aunt Rachel (Mr Wardle's spinster sister) enters:

> PICKWICK: Oh, lord! [*Starts up and peeps through curtain. Tableaux.* (See plate, No.8) *With astonishment*] It's a female Dick Turpin! I will alarm the house! [*Aside*][39]

The picture is evidently the same as Phiz's 'The middle-aged lady in the double-bedded room' in Chapter 22 of the novel; the scene is the same and the consequences are in many ways similar (Pickwick has to face the authority of the law in the form of special constable Daniel Grummer). However, the crucial difference is that, in the novel, the 'middle-aged lady' is not Aunt Rachel but Miss Witherfield (who is to be betrothed to Mr Magnus). Stirling omits both Magnus and Witherfield, presumably in an attempt to impose a manageable dramatic shape on to Dickens's sprawling narrative. The difference might seem to be a minor one but, taken together with the many other similar examples which occur throughout the early adaptations, it raises questions about exactly how the audience perceived the relationship between the original novel and the stage version.

The use of the illustration-tableau would suggest the expectation of audience familiarity with the serial instalments of the novels themselves: the pleasure to be gained through such acts of mimicry could only be brought about by an instant recognition of the similarities. At the same time, however, the assumption of the audience's intimate acquaintance with the text would suggest that dramatists were also aware that any deviation from or alteration of the original narrative would immediately be recognised. If this is the case, one can argue that contemporary enjoyment of Dickens adaptations was founded upon the recognition of both similarity and difference. This would in turn imply that the audience's engagement with the plays was far more active and, in its own way, sophisticated than some contemporary critics alleged.[40] Even in the published versions of the plays, what might at first seem like simple plagiarism could in fact be a more playful and self-conscious means of alerting the reader to the ambiguous relationship between novel and adaptation. Thus, as was the case with many published versions of these plays, Edward Stirling's *The Fortunes of Smike* was 'splendidly illustrated with an etching by Pierce Egan, the Younger, from a drawing taken during the representation'.[41] Egan's 'illustration' is, in fact, virtually an exact copy of Phiz's illustration for Chapter 58 of the novel, which is entitled 'The recognition' and depicts Smike, during his last illness, as he sees a shadowy figure watching him from beneath the shade of a tree. At one level this is simple theft; at another it is a faithful record of a dramatic performance in which Phiz's 'The recognition' was painstakingly recreated on stage. The main difference between the illustrations is that Egan's version has a standardised proscenium arch border which alerts the reader to the fact that the action illustrated should be imagined as taking place upon the stage; or, to put this another way, it acts as a reminder of the fact that the plate is not a copy of Phiz's illustration but a new illustration of the dramatisation of the original. (The new engraving literally depicts the old illustration put on the stage.) When the two plates are placed together, however, what one becomes aware of is not, paradoxically, the similarity between them but, rather, the differences which are highlighted because of the general similarity. The effect is somewhat like a child's 'spot the difference' game in which two nearly identical pictures are placed side by side. One becomes aware, for example, of a female figure missing in the background, of the different ways in which clothing or facial expressions are represented. The audience in the theatre or the reader of the published play wanted to reexperience a novel that they had enjoyed but, at the same time, they wanted something new; they wanted to recognise a text with which they were familiar (as they recognised the tableau scenes or Egan's reproduction of Phiz's engraving) but, simultaneously, they wanted that recognition to be the starting point for further, different entertainment. The following section of the present chapter will return to William Moncrieff and examine the different nature of the entertainment he provided in his adaptation of the *Pickwick Papers* as *Sam Weller, or, the Pickwickians*.

ONE OF THE SPECIFIC SCENES from *Pickwick Papers* referred to in Forster's scathing *Examiner* review of Moncrieff's adaptation of the novel is the election episode in the fictitious town of Eatanswill. 'Who,' writes Forster, 'that has perused the graphic description of a contested election in the *Pickwick Papers* ... can recognise a solitary trait ... in the boisterous pantomime of the half-dozen miserable supernumeraries of a minor theatre?'[42] More recently, however, James Vernon, in a study of electoral practice in the period, has observed that it 'is possible to read the narrative of electoral rites as a melodramatic text(s) through which constituencies literally acted out the various generic plots of romance, comedy, tragedy, and irony'.[43] Vernon proceeds to highlight a number of ways in which contemporary elections could be seen as ritualised performances which engaged not just candidates, officials and voters but the entire constituency – both franchised and disenfranchised. It might be assumed from this that the election scene in *Pickwick Papers* would be eminently suited for dramatic representation and this is, indeed, suggested by an examination of Dickens's original text. Not only is the episode full of references to the performance of music and the use of visual props such as flags and banners, there is also continued reference to the theatricality of the participants' behaviour. Thus Dickens writes that Mr Pott 'melodramatically testified by gestures to the crowd, his ineffaceable obligations to the Eatanswill Gazette'.[44] Slightly later, a 'little choleric, pink-faced man' stands forward in order to propose a candidate and is similarly seen to resort, out of necessity, to the strategies of popular theatre:

> after a very few sentences of figurative eloquence, the pink-faced gentleman got from denouncing those who interrupted him in the mob, to exchanging defiances with the gentlemen on the hustings; whereupon arose an uproar which reduced him to the necessity of expressing his feelings by serious pantomime, which he did, and then left the stage to his seconder, who delivered a written speech of half an hour's length. (p. 252)

An election would seem to be an occasion where 'figurative eloquence' and the power of the 'written' word have to give way to the broader appeal of melodramatic utterance and pantomimic gesture. Dickens's text, of course, contains the potential excesses of such discourse within the bounds of his own written eloquence: Forster might refer to the 'graphic' quality of the scene in the novel, but it is the novelist's skills as a writer which the reader responds to and which construct an artistic order through which the chaos of the election is perceived. In the theatre, on the other hand, this element of artistic control is less explicit and, it could be argued, more ambiguous. In his study of actual electoral practice, Vernon argues that

> oral media of this period, much like their visual counterparts, afforded their audiences and participants considerable power in shaping the terms in which politics was articulated. This is not to argue that oral media could not be used in restrictive ways, but rather that generally their use facilitated more expansive and inclusive definitions of the political subject and the public political sphere. ... (T)he increasing use of print as a mode of political communication slowly began to eclipse the use of oral and visual media and, in the process, placed greater emphasis on the individual's private experience of politics.[45]

Dickens's written account of the election provides a detached and 'private' experience of electoral practice. A theatrical representation, however, which literalised the melodramatic and pantomimic metaphors of Dickens's text, would have the potential to address what Vernon terms 'more expansive and inclusive' notions of political involvement.

Dickens's election is ostensibly set in 1827 or 1828 (the second of these two dates is the one mentioned in the chapter itself) and so, in many ways, it can be seen to depict the corruptions present in the electoral system prior to the Reform Act of 1832. Having said this, it is evident that electoral abuses continued and it is generally accepted that Dickens was drawing upon his own first-hand experience of, for example, elections at Sudbury and Ipswich when he came to write his account.[46] None the less, the descriptions are, on the whole, generalised: the satire is broad rather than specific and the two parties of 'Blue' and 'Buff', Slumkey and Fizkin, are hardly differentiated in terms of political affiliation or belief. The chapter in which the scene occurs was published in serial form in August 1836; Moncrieff's *Sam Weller* was probably first performed on 10 July 1837.[47] On 20 June 1837 the king, William IV, died (to be succeeded by Victoria), an event which constitutionally occasioned the need for a general election. Parliament was dissolved on 17 July, elections took place over the summer and the new parliament met for the first time in the November of 1837. The Whigs, who were in power under the leadership of Lord Melbourne, had already, in 1835, lost many of the seats gained in the 1832 post-Reform Election and this trend was to continue, with the Tories, under Peel, becoming, in the words of Norman Gash, 'a more powerful Opposition than any known before'.[48] The 1837 general election was, therefore extremely hard-fought and it is in the context of this election fever, with a Whig government desperately attempting to prevent further losses to an increasingly confident Tory party, that the election scene in Moncrieff's *Sam Weller* was being performed.

The most striking thing that is noticed about Moncrieff's adaptation of this episode is the way in which it turns the election into one which is explicitly fought in terms of a clash between Whigs and Tories:

WARDLE: Come along, girls – come along – rare bustling scene, 'faith – never saw so great a party spirit, in so small a place, in my life – Buff and Blue – they'll buffet one another, till they're black and blue, before they've done, or I'm very much mistaken – one half of them will really be in buff, and the other half, looking very blue indeed. Well, I shall vote for the liberal party.

ISABELLA: You know I'm for freedom of speech, pa. Right of election! – purity of choice! – choosing one's own representative! – and everything of that kind!

WARDLE: You're a Radical, you madcap, you are. What are your principles, Emily?

EMILY: I would be more exclusive, sir! – as Mr. Snodgrass says – the institutions of our forefathers should be preserved inviolate – I disclaim innovation, and would have no changes in the state – everything should remain just as it is!

ISABELLA: Mercy on me, Emily! I'd change my state directly, if I could – I don't want to remain as I am by any means – nor does Mr. Winkle – or I'm very much mistaken – True Blue forever!

EMILY: Orange – the peerless Orange for me!

DUET. – Isabella and Emily
Air. – 'Hurrah! for the Red and the Blue.'

> Hurrah! for the Buff and the Blue,
> May they both to their Monarch prove true,
> Be staunch to the cause,
> Of our Charter and Laws,
> And while raising the glories,
> Of Whigs and of Tories,
> Still keep England's welfare in view!

WARDLE: Well said – never quarrel about politics, girls![49]

The terms of the actual election are briefly rehearsed by Emily and Isabella: the Whig and Radical causes are conflated to form a party of reform and change, the Tories are seen to be the party of a quasi-Burkean adherence to the *status quo*. And yet, whilst the world of 'real' political debate is seemingly allowed into the world of the play, there is evidently at the same time an attempt to reduce any appearance of an overtly political intervention. The differences between the parties are expressed by young female characters who are seen simply to be mouthing the views of their lovers. Moreover, the language of political will soon becomes translated into that of amorous intent as Isabella turns her 'radical' desire to alter the state into a wish that her own single 'state' could be transformed into a married one. Such banter, which goes some way to defuse the political content of the speeches, is appositely concluded by the duet which explicitly puts aside the issue of party politics and celebrates instead a sense of national identity and tradition which ostensibly lies beyond party bias. What Moncrieff seemingly does, then, is present a stable notion of the nation in which Whigs and Tories can compete for power without essentially changing the political *status quo*: the 'Monarch', 'Charter' and 'Laws' remain inviolate. Any radically dissenting voices are restricted to comic illiterate or drunken members of the crowd, such as the 'Drunken Liberal', 'Match Seller' and 'Ballad Singer' who cry out for 'uniwersal suffering', 'triangular Parleyments – and wote by ballad'.[50] Such manglings of the demands of early Chartism would seem effectively to deny their significance in the world presented by the play.

However, the need to gain a licence to perform the play would mean that, particularly during a general election, any political references would have to be very carefully handled and that the appearance of any reformist tendencies would have to be rigorously suppressed. As one examines the scene in more detail, one becomes aware of a certain bias in Moncrieff's representation of the contemporary political scene. The first indication of this is, of course, the fact that Pickwick and Sam are supporters of Slumkey who, in Moncrieff's version, is the Whig candidate. Audience sympathy evidently lies with these characters whose election chorus explicitly associates the Whig cause with liberal reform:

Enter in Procession, MR PICKWICK, the HONOURABLE MR SLUMKEY, of Slumkey Hall, MR TUPMAN, DRUNKEN LIBERAL, and Slumkey's party, male and female, with favours, &c.
CHORUS. – Sam and Slumkey's party.
Air. – 'Hurrah for the bonnets of blue!'

    Here's a health to the Friends of Reform,
    Electors who're honest and true;
    And may those who will not vote for Eatanswill's good,
    Like our colours be made to look blue!
    'Tis good to be Liberal Whigs,
    'Tis good to be honest and true;
    'Tis good to support noble Slumkey's cause,
    And vote for the Triumph of Blue!
    Hurrah, &c.

(Pickwick and Slumkey ascend the Hustings.)[51]

Unlike the novel, here Sam and Pickwick are allowed to profess a specific political allegiance which is inevitably designed to be sympathised with by the audience who are also expected to be, one has to assume, 'Friends of Reform'. In contrast, Fizkin's Tory Party is presented in an extremely negative fashion. The main vehicle for this, again in a departure from the novel, are the characters of Jingle and Job Trotter who, in the guise of Captain Fitztory and servant, have aligned themselves (for inevitably selfish ends) with the Tory candidate. As Trotter puts it, Jingle has 'turned Conservative – advocates Aristocratic principles – and has managed to become head Committee-man to Horatio Fizkin'.[52] Whilst Jingle and Trotter are evidently also deceiving Fizkin himself, the Tory cause within the play is necessarily linked with their own greed and deception. The pair of conmen fall behind the Tory campaign with relish, as Trotter indicates: 'capital gag, our calling Slumkey's party the Destructives – volunteering to preserve the people's property – gad, if it once comes into our hands, we'll take care of it, with a witness to it'.[53] As Jingle's assumed name of Fitztory suggests, the crooked duo really do seem to 'fit' the 'Tories'.

In contrast to the positive and celebratory Whig song, the procession and chorus of the Tories is full of irony:

Enter R., in Procession, the other side, HORATIO FIZKIN, ESQ., MAYOR, CRYER, JINGLE, TROTTER, and their party.
CHORUS. – Trotter and Fizkin's Party.
Air. – 'March, march, Ettrick and Teviotdale.'

> March, march, Destructives and Radicals.
> Break their heads lads, you who're friends to good order;
> March, march, Democrats and Jacobins,
> Make their Blue Colours yield to the Recorder!
> Many a Freeholder,
> Many a be-holder,
> We have addressed, with the old Tory story;
> Shout, and in Eatanswill,
> You shall have all your fill,
> Let the Blue Party be thrown in disorder!
> March, march &c.

(Mayor and Cryer take centre place – Fizkin and Jingle ascend the Hustings.)[54]

There is no attempt here to present a 'positive' message: the Tory propaganda works solely through its attacks upon the opposition and the threat of violence or bribery. Trotter has already explained to the audience the significance of the term 'Destructives' as a constructed term of abuse, but the song ironically highlights that it is more suitable as a name for the Tories whose vision of 'good order' is the breaking of heads. However, the audience might also be aware of Bronterre O'Brien's radical working-class newspaper, *The Destructive*.[55] In this context, the use of this name, together with the highly politicised terms 'radical', 'democrat' and 'Jacobin', becomes extremely problematic in that the radicalism they suggest is made to appear more attractive than the hypocritical self-advancement represented by the singers of the present 'Chorus'. Perhaps even more significant is the fact that the Tory 'party' as represented by the procession includes the Mayor and the Cryer who, in Dickens's novel, are clearly the impartial mediating officials in the election process. Whilst Mayor and Cryer move away from the Tory party once the procession reaches the hustings, the impression given to the theatre audience is that the 'Tories' here are the party of the establishment whereas the 'Whigs' represent a more oppositional force belonging to the 'people'. (After Slumkey's victory, Isabella exclaims, 'I told you sir! the people would win – another victory in the cause of the population!'[56]) That the Whigs were the party in power in 1837 is in many ways irrelevant: what the play seems to depict is a bias towards the reform of traditional power structures which still rely upon the 'old Tory story' and its innate corruption.

Furthermore, throughout the scene it is the Tories who are associated with violence and aggression. After the election celebrations, Pickwick and his friends return to the stage:

Enter PICKWICK and TUPMAN, covered with mud and dust – and SAM, with a black eye, and his nose damaged.

PICKWICK: Confound the villains – Exclusives do they call themselves – I wish they'd been a little more exclusive, with their kicks and cuffs – a queer way of polling theirs – cracked heads as plenty as blackberries. But, however, we're not so bad off as the Honourable Slumkey – for they've soused him in the horse-pond.

SAM: Rayther a rough scramble, sir, certainly – but I paid a few on 'em
– and gave the t'others a receipt – I'll jist rub you down a bit, with
this ere jack towel, vhat I borrow'd from the cook – and then see if I
can't cork up my claret, here, a little.

(Sam rubs down Pickwick and Tupman.)

WARDLE: Are these the lofty principles of your high-minded elevated
party, Emily? – knocking everybody down.
PICKWICK: What, my dear friend Wardle, Emily, and Isabella, too! – I
rejoice to meet you – don't stare – Tupman and I have only been rolled
in the kennel for the good of the country.
WARDLE: One half of our patriots should be served in the same way.
TUPMAN: I haven't a whole bone left in my body – if this is your march
of intellect – to be run over, and trod by every blackguard in the
country – I've done.
SAM *(Finishing rubbing them down)*: There, sir! – there you are. Now I'll
go and perform my toilet.

[Exit Sam

WARDLE: Well – well – well! – I rejoice that your man has come in,
however. He is a Liberal – and while we return such members as he
is, the cause of Liberty and Old England must flourish![57]

In the speech quoted earlier, Emily talks of her belief in a more
'exclusive' politics, by which she means a limited franchise and the
restriction of political power; here, the 'Exclusives' are revealed to
be nothing other than the thugs celebrated in the Tory election
song. Outside the world of the play, the term 'Exclusives' seems to
have had some currency in the early years of the 1830s following
the anonymous publication, in 1830, of a novel entitled *The
Exclusives* by Lady Charlotte Bury. The novel casts a satirical look
at an upper-class coterie grouped around the figure of a Lady Tilney
who woos young politicians in order to exert an influence in the
public sphere. In the novel itself, Lady Tilney's politics are of a
hypocritical Whiggish variety: 'She, indeed, was one of those
haughty liberals who affect to despise kings and courts; not because
they dislike those necessary evils, as they call them, but because
they are themselves, or would be if they could, the greatest of all
sovereigns.'[58] Political affiliations were in a state of flux during
this decade, however, and, by 1837, it is quite possible that such
'exclusive' politics were just as readily associated with the kind of

exclusive and essentially Whiggish *salon* organised by Lady Blessington of which the dandyish young poet, novelist and Radical-turned-Tory Benjamin Disraeli was also a member.[59] Disraeli was, of course, first elected to parliament (after four unsuccessful attempts), as member for Maidstone, in the 1837 elections. Within the play, the association of such 'exclusive' Toryism with the dandified figure of the poet Snodgrass begins to have a deeper resonance when it is put into the context of the kind of elitist aesthetic and political coterie grouped around figures such as Lady Blessington. Wardle's final speech returns the play to an apparently anodyne celebration of 'Liberty and Old England', but the Liberalism which he extols is one which opposes 'exclusivity', of either the Tory or the Whig variety, with the kind of 'inclusive' politics that Vernon describes.

When Wardle ironically asks Emily about the 'lofty principles' of her 'high-minded elevated party', the audience is given a clear message about the dangerous duplicity of the politics of exclusion. At the same time, one is reminded of Moncrieff's attack on the (for him) similarly hypocritical *Examiner*'s 'high intellectual' school of criticism which he saw as committing a kind of metaphorical violence upon the literary 'opposition' through aggressive and biased reviewing. In this light, it is perhaps significant to note that Forster himself was also associated with the Blessington circle, particularly through his friendships with writers such as Edward Bulwer-Lytton and Letitia Landon. In the present scene Tupman exclaims against the cliched 'march of intellect'. Such complaints were often directed against an increasingly educated and therefore politicised working class: Asa Briggs, for example, notes that 'Lord Eldon is claimed to have believed that the march of mind would one day or the other direct "a hundred thousand tall fellows with clubs and pikes against Whitehall"'. Here, however, it is directed against the social exclusivity and elitism represented in the play by the Tories. None the less, radicals too could be suspicious of the dangers of intellectualism: Briggs also records that 'Cobbett thundered against "Scotch feelosophy" and education by too many books'.[60] The fact, then, that the *Examiner*'s politics were liberal is, in this instance, immaterial. The entry in the *Dictionary of National Biography* for its editor Albany Fonblanque describes it as 'the chief organ of high-class intellectual radicalism'.[61] Moncrieff might possibly have supported the 'radicalism', but he evidently would have had difficulty accepting the 'high-class intellectual' aspect of the periodical and those associated with it. It would seem that, for Moncrieff, both 'high intellectual' criticism and the 'march of intellect' worked to counter the popular choice of the people – be it in politics or literature. What emerges is an anti-intellectual populism which becomes one of the standard defences of 'popular' culture.

The conclusion to Moncrieff's play again takes its audience into the realms of contemporary public life by having Pickwick, who is newly released from prison, accompany his friends to the celebrations brought about by the Accession of Queen Victoria. Again, it would be possible to read this as an act of conservative nationalism, with the final memory of the play's performance being the protagonists' cries of 'God save the Queen' and the splendour of a 'Procession of Heralds, Beefeaters, Guards &c.' who pass through Temple Bar 'amidst general shouts of joy and congratulations'.[62] In the political world of 1837, however, even such apparently simple patriotism could be seen to have a political inflection, particularly in light of the seemingly pro-Whig/Liberal bias of the earlier election scene. Victoria was known to have a personal liking for Melbourne (the Whig prime minister) which meant that her accession caused considerable problems for the Tories. Norman Gash observes that 'Victoria's adolescent attachment to Melbourne, and by extension her emotional though not intellectual adherence to the Whigs, created unusual difficulties for the only possible alternative Ministry. The effects of the Queen's name in the elections of 1837 and 1841 became a factor in the calculations of party electioneering experts, and her relationship with the Prime Minister in those of the party leaders.'[63] Seen in these terms, therefore, the celebration of Victoria could be calculated to bolster an anti-Tory campaign. None the less, it would perhaps be wrong to attempt to ascribe too specific a political agenda to Moncrieff's play. Both the accession scene and the earlier election episode are reluctant to reveal an explicit political ideology and, despite the possibility of detecting a potential bias against the Tories, the play remains largely ambiguous in this respect. What can be asserted, however, is that, unlike Dickens's novel, Moncrieff's play allows explicitly political ideas to circulate within the performed text and, moreover, that they circulate in a fashion which is less easy to contain than it would be within a written text. In a comparison of written with oral or graphic texts, James Vernon notes that 'unlike print there was ... a sense in which the audience were not just receivers, but effective producers of these more flexible and visual texts'.[64] This element of participation, which the songs, music and spectacle of the theatre encouraged, provides the element of 'difference' demanded by the audience of a Dickens adaptation. Whilst the characters (and often their dialogue) are essentially the same, they have moved more obviously into the world of the audience's lived experience, and their actions and decisions have become more explicitly involved with the uncertainties of contemporary society.

IN AN ESSAY ON THE class ideology of *Oliver Twist*, Bill Bell positions Dickens the professional novelist within the rapidly changing social structures of the 1830s. He takes issue with previous readings of Dickens's early work which have attempted to place the writer in a 'privileged' position beyond or above the realm of class politics. 'As a member of the same middle-class as many of his readers,' Bell writes, 'Dickens's social profile in 1837 is hardly one that can be described as perpetually privileged; the author of *Oliver Twist* can, on the contrary, be seen at this stage in his career at least as a new kind of representative writer for a new kind of reading public.' He continues to observe that critics have often failed to note the 'crucial aspect of lower/middle class *ambiguity* that epitomised the phenomenal rise of "Boz"'.[65] This 'ambiguity' can be offered as a possible cause for Dickens's fear of shabby gentility or his worries about the 'vulgarity' of theatrical adaptations of his work over which he had no control. Moncrieff's adaptations perhaps offered a particular threat, first because of the unwelcome associations the author of *Tom and Jerry* brought with him and, second (as has been seen from the internal evidence of *Sam Weller*), because of the ways in which his plays allowed for a more 'inclusive' popular politics than Dickens's role as 'a new kind of representative writer' for the aspiring middle classes could allow.

Discussing the emergence of the independent professional writer in the early decades of the nineteenth century, Norman Feltes argues that many accounts have been 'dazzled by Dickens's

£93,000 legacy' and are thus only able to celebrate unconditionally the new situation of the author. In contrast, Feltes emphasises the 'precariousness of the writer's new position within the publishers' new structures for controlling the production of books' and describes how the author, 'genius or hack, presented himself [*sic*] to the publisher, as did any other worker in the capitalist mode of production, as 'the owner of nothing but his labour-power'''.[66] What Feltes might add, however, is that the value of a writer's 'labour-power' within the capitalist mode of production is dependent upon how they present themselves in the marketplace. Whilst, as a system, capitalism might not differentiate between 'genius' and 'hack', in terms of marketing oneself within the system the difference is crucial. As has been seen, Moncrieff had attempted to argue for the equivalence of himself and Dickens as writers whose financial wellbeing was dependent upon the commodity value of their literary productions. However, Dickens had already, in the 'literary gentleman' episode of *Nicholas Nickleby*, made a clear distinction between 'genius' and 'hack' and it was evident that, as far as Dickens was concerned, Moncrieff would never be able to assert his credentials as a writer worthy of serious attention. That he is solely remembered now, if at all, as the source for Dickens's satirical portrait of the adapter of novels, attests to the power of the social changes which both he and Dickens worked within.

Notes

1 The authoritative guide to adaptations of Dickens's work is H. Philip Bolton, *Dickens Dramatized* (London, Mansell Publishing, 1987).

2 See the letter to Frederick Yates (dating from mid-March 1838) in which Dickens writes, 'Supposing we arrange preliminaries for our mutual satisfaction, I propose to dramatize Oliver for the first night of next Season', in Dickens, *The Pilgrim Edition of The Letters of Charles Dickens, Volume One 1820–1839*, ed. Madeline House and Graham Storey (Oxford, Clarendon Press, 1965), p. 388. The plan was never put into practice – see the editors' notes to the edition of the *Letters* cited above.

3 John Forster, *The Life of Charles Dickens, Volume One 1812–1842* (London, Chapman and Hall, 1872), p. 152. John Glavin sums up Dickens's ambivalence towards the theatre by claiming that 'from the start Dickens was in not quite equal parts thrilled (less) and (more)

frightened by the stage', in *After Dickens: Reading, Adaptation and Performance* (Cambridge, Cambridge University Press, 1999), p. 11.

4 For an account of Dickens's desire for control in all aspects of his professional life, see Grahame Smith, *Charles Dickens: A Literary Life* (London, Macmillan, 1996), pp. 6–8.

5 Dickens, 'Shabby-genteel people', first published in the *Morning Chronicle*, 5 November 1834 as 'Street sketches No. 4', *Sketches by Boz*, Volume Two, February 1836. Text taken from Michael Slater (ed.), *Dickens's Journalism: Sketches By Boz and Other Early Papers 1833–39* (London, J. M. Dent, 1994), p. 262.

6 Dickens, 'Shabby-genteel people', p. 264.

7 By far the best account of the origins of Pickwick from this perspective is to be found in Robert L. Patten, *Charles Dickens and His Publishers* (Oxford, Clarendon Press, 1978), Chapter 3 passim.

8 Kathryn Chittick, *Dickens and the 1830s* (Cambridge, Cambridge University Press, 1990). See, for example, p. 91: 'If later critics have tried to explain away many of *Pickwick*'s structural peculiarities according to the categories of the novel, without considering the appropriateness of their models, it is at least in part because Dickens and his closest colleagues deliberately set the first example. *Pickwick* may not have been a novel in its original idea or composition, but by the end of its run nearly two years later ... Dickens had decided that he was going to be known as a novelist'.

9 See, for example, Patten, *Dickens and His Publishers*, pp. 53–4 and Bolton, *Dickens Dramatized*, pp. 23–4.

10 Playbill included in Thomas Hailes Lacy's edition of *The Pickwickians; or The Peregrinations of Sam Weller. A Comic Drama, In Three Acts. Arranged from Moncrieff's Adaptation of Charles Dickens' Work*, by T. H. Lacy (London, Lacy, ?1837). H. Philip Bolton's observations are worth noting here: 'Just as Pierce Egan's book was one precedent on which the *Pickwick Papers* themselves were poised, so the dramatic versions of *Life in London* were leaps from the page to the boards that Moncrieff and others had practised on Egan's novel before they came to Dickens's' (*Dickens Dramatized*, p. 23).

11 Letter to Frederick Yates (?29 November 1838), Dickens, *Letters, Volume One*, p. 463.

12 Marilyn Gaull, one of the few recent critics to discuss Moncrieff's work, describes it as displaying 'a remarkable sensitivity to dramatic fashion and an equally remarkable facility in adapting to the stage the novels that were serialized in magazines, sometimes before the install-

ments were finished', in *English Romanticism: The Human Context* (New York and London, W. W. Norton, 1988), p. 94.

13 Deborah Vlock notes: 'The probability that novelists, like Dickens, whose serial fiction was regularly plagiarized, were forced to dance with hack playwrights as they wrote, requires us to rethink our relationship to these texts', in *Dickens, Novel Reading, and the Victorian Popular Theatre* (Cambridge, Cambridge University Press, 1998), p. 4.

14 *Report from the Select Committee on Dramatic Literature: with The Minutes of Evidence.* Ordered by the House of Commons to be Printed, 2 August 1832. (Dublin, Irish University Press, 1968), p. 176.

15 W. T. Moncrieff, *Poems*, Printed (For Private Distribution Only) at the Author's Private Address, Saville House, Lambeth, 1829, unnumbered page.

16 See the archives of the Royal Literary Fund, File Number 1008. Moncrieff was give £25 by the RLF as a result of his petition. One of his sponsors, Sir Lumley St George Skeffington, wrote that Moncrieff was 'a gentleman of acknowledged literary taste, and high honour'. In 1831, Moncrieff had acted as a sponsor for a young writer named George McCaul. With his letter he included a copy of his own volume of poems: 'allow me,' he writes, 'as a very humble member of the "writing public" to beg your acceptance of a little volume, printed for private and gratuitous distribution only, thus providing with a wide caution, not usual in authors, against any chance of disappointment in its sale.' Moncrieff continued to think of the *Poems* as a sign of his literary respectability: as late as 1851, when, totally blind, he was living in the Charterhouse, he sent a copy as a gift to Benjamin Guy Babbington (see the MS letter and poem in one of the British Library copies of the volume). It is interesting to note, in light of the general argument of the present chapter, that Pierce Egan's request for financial support from the RLF in 1830 was rejected because, as a file note observes, 'his writings have been deemed of an improper tendency' (see File Number 686).

17 W. T. Moncrieff, *The March of Intellect, A Comic Poem* (London, William Kidd and Charles Tilt, 1830), pp. 21–2. The poem is accompanied with six designs by Robert Cruikshank. The theme and title are, of course, significant given the later discussion of the 'march of intellect' in the present chapter.

18 W. T. Moncrieff, *Ivanhoe! or, The Jewess. A Chivalric Play, in Three Acts; Founded on the Popular Romance of 'Ivanhoe'* (London, Lowndes and Marshall, 1820), unnumbered page. It will be remembered that Scott did provide proofs to his friend Daniel Terry for the purposes outlined by Moncrieff.

19 Review of numbers 19 and 20 of *Pickwick Papers* in *Examiner*, 1553, 5 November 1837, p. 708.

20 *Examiner*, 1537, 16 July 1837, p. 454.

21 W. T. Moncrieff, *Sam Weller, or, the Pickwickians. A Drama, in Three Acts, As Performed at the New Strand Theatre, with Unexampled Success* ... (London, Published for the Author. And Sold by all respectable Booksellers, 1837), pp. iii–iv. On the 'undramatic' nature of Pickwick Papers see also the 'Advertisement' to William Leman Rede's adaptation, Peregrinations of Pickwick: 'The unfitness of the Papers for the purposes of the drama, I believed ere I began this task, and know now. This version was written when only the eighth number of the Papers was published', in *Peregrinations of Pickwick; A Drama, in Three Acts* (London, Strange, 1837), unnumbered page.

22 Moncrieff, *Sam Weller*, pp. iv–v. The *Examiner* was published on a Sunday – hence Moncrieff's reference to its 'Sunday-school of criticism'.

23 Moncrieff, *Sam Weller*, p. vii.

24 Letter to Forster, 7 September 1837, Dickens, *Letters, Volume One*, p. 304. Moncrieff describes himself as a member of the dramatic authors' society on the title page of *Sam Weller*.

25 *Examiner*, 17 September 1837, p. 599.

26 Dickens, *Nicholas Nickleby* (London, Penguin Popular Classics, 1994), p. 623.

27 Dickens, *Nicholas Nickleby*, p. 624.

28 Dickens, *Nicholas Nickleby*, p. 625.

29 Moncrieff, 'To the Public', quoted in full in S. J. Adair Fitz-Gerald, *Dickens and the Drama, Being an Account of Charles Dickens's Connections with the Stage and the Stage's Connection with Him* ... (London, Chapman and Hall, 1910), p. 121.

30 Moncrieff, 'To the Public', p. 125.

31 Unsigned notice, 'Charles Dickens and his works', *Fraser's Magazine*, April 1840, xxi, 381–400, quoted in Philip Collins (ed.), *Dickens: The Critical Heritage* (London, Routledge, 1971), p. 89.

32 Unsigned review of *Oliver Twist*, in the *Literary Gazette*, 24 November 1838, p. 741, quoted in Collins (ed.), *Dickens*, p. 79.

33 [Thomas Cleghorn?], from 'Writings of Charles Dickens', *North British Review*, May 1845, iii, pp 65–87, quoted in Collins (ed.) *Dickens*, p. 191.

34 [Thomas Cleghorn?], from 'Writings of Charles Dickens', p. 190.

35 It is interesting to note that modern commentators on the illustrations to Dickens's novels feel the need to resort to a version of the 'depth'

model of hidden meaning when they discuss the importance of the visual art. Thus, for example, Michael Steig writes:

> I have uncovered no evidence of how subtly contemporary readers 'read' Browne's illustrations, nor do we have access to Browne's or Dickens' thoughts on the matter ... Even if not a single Victorian reader recognised the complexities of the texts; they are at once the expression of Dickens' intentions and Browne's interpretations, at once a visual accompaniment to the text and a commentary upon it. They were important to Dickens, and they can be important to any reader who makes the effort to recapture a mode of 'reading' graphic art which may already have been dying out in the mid-nineteenth century.

(In *Dickens and Phiz* (Bloomington, IN and London, Indiana University Press, 1978), p. 5.)

36 Grahame Smith observes that 'it could be argued that despite the control [Dickens] exerted over Phiz's illustrations, they constitute an element of adaptation from within the text itself', in 'Dickens and adaptation: imagery in words and pictures', in Peter Reynolds (ed.), *Novel Images: Literature in Performance* (London, Routledge, 1993), p. 52.

37 Bolton, *Dickens Dramatized*, pp. 155–6.

38 W. T. Moncrieff, *Tom and Jerry; or , Life in London: An Operatic Extravaganza* (London, Richardson and Penny; Edinburgh, Hunter; Paris, Truchy, 1828), p. vi.

39 Edward Stirling, *The Pickwick Club: or, The Age We Live In! A Burletta in Three Acts* (London, Duncombe, 1837), p. 44.

40 The twentieth-century critic Deborah Vlock observes: 'Out of the concords and discords of these competing texts evolved what I would call an "imaginary text" – the actual Dickens experience, overdetermined, centered not as much in any one narrative or genre but in the theatre of assumptions among the London public', in *Dickens, Novel Reading, and the Victorian Popular Theatre*, p. 79. Whilst I would agree with the general point here, I would argue for a more active and discriminating audience participation in the production of textual meaning(s) than Vlock perhaps implies. And it should also be noted (though I too fail to address the issue in the present book) that the 'theatre of assumptions' had a national if not international dimension and was certainly not limited to the 'London public'.

41 Edward Stirling, *The Fortunes of Smike, or a Sequel to Nicholas Nickleby* (London, Sherwood, Gilbert and Piper, no date; play first performed at the Adelphi, 2 March 1840). The play is not a 'sequel' to the novel but an adaptation of the second half, beginning with Nicholas already engaged as a professional actor. It is more properly

a 'sequel' to Stirling's earlier adaptation, *Nicholas Nickleby; or Doings at Do-the-boys Hall* which had opened in 1838 during the early months of serial publication and for which Stirling had, inevitably, provided his own narrative resolution. The presence of Pierce Egan, the Younger as illustrator for the present adaptation only serves to underline the interconnectedness of the literary scene.

42 *Examiner*, 1537, 16 July 1837, p. 454.

43 James Vernon, *Politics and the People: A Study in English Political Culture, c. 1815–1867* (Cambridge, Cambridge University Press, 1993), p. 80.

44 Charles Dickens, *The Pickwick Papers*, ed. Robert L. Patten (London, Penguin, 1972), p. 249. All references are to this edition.

45 Vernon, *Politics and the People*, p. 131.

46 For the 1835 Sudbury election, see, for example, Asa Briggs, *The Age of Improvement 1783–1867* (London, Longman, 1959), p. 266.

47 Bolton gives a one-off 'opening' performance of 'ca 12 June', apparently working back from a later playbill (Bolton, *Dickens Dramatized*, p. 78); other sources (DNB entry for Moncrieff; Chadwyck-Healey *English Verse Drama* database) consistently state 10 July as the first performance; and the date of Forster's review in the Sunday *Examiner* (16 July) would suggest that he was reviewing a new play that he had seen that week. The play stayed on the playbills of the Strand Theatre until 12 October, the end of the season. It is quite possible, of course, that the play was altered during the course of its run to accommodate contemporary events: the published version used here ends with a scene set during the accession of Queen Victoria which has to have been written after the death of William IV on 20 June and so could not have been included in Bolton's first performance.

48 Norman Gash, *Reaction and Reconstruction: English Politics 1832–1852* (Oxford, Clarendon Press, 1965), p. 145; on the political context, see also Peter Mandler, *Aristocratic Government in the Age of Reform: Whigs and Liberals, 1830–1852* (Oxford, Clarendon Press, 1990), especially, pp. 167–8.

49 Moncrieff, *Sam Weller*, II.ii, pp. 59–60.

50 Moncrieff, *Sam Weller*, II.ii, p. 57; Moncrieff seemingly steals the first two puns from Stirling's earlier adaptation (see Stirling, *The Pickwick Club*, p. 31. Stirling's play was first performed on 27 April 1837 at the City of London Theatre).

51 Moncrieff, *Sam Weller*, II.ii, p. 63.

52 Moncrieff, *Sam Weller*, II.ii, p. 58.

53 Moncrieff, *Sam Weller*, II.ii, p. 59.

54 Moncrieff, *Sam Weller*, II.ii, pp. 63–4.

55 See E. P. Thomson, *The Making of the English Working Class* (rev. edn, Harmondsworth, Penguin, 1968), p. 800.

56 Moncrieff, *Sam Weller*, II.ii, p. 68.

57 Moncrieff, *Sam Weller*, II.iii, pp. 68–70.

58 [Lady Charlotte Bury], *The Exclusives* (3rd edn, London, Colburn and Bentley, 1830), p. 6. I am indebted to Steven Earnshaw and Peter Cain for their help in tracking down the possible significance of the 'Exclusives' within Moncrieff's play.

59 See, for example, Robert Blake, *Disraeli* (London, Eyre and Spottiswoode, 1966), p. 113: 'He dined regularly with Lady Blessington at Gore House. D'Orsay was his friend, and he writes in his diary: "I am as popular with the first-rate men as I am hated by the second-rate".' D'Orsay was 'the dandy of the day ... who lived with the widowed second wife of the last Earl of Blessington in circumstances which occasioned much scandal' (p. 79).

60 Briggs, *The Age of Improvement*, p. 224

61 Leslie Stephen (ed.), *Dictionary of National Biography* (London, Smith, Elder, 1889), Vol. XIX, p. 364. The entry is by Richard Garnett.

62 Moncrieff, *Sam Weller*, Scene the Last, p. 153.

63 Gash, *Reaction and Reconstruction*, pp. 22–3.

64 Vernon, *Politics and The People*, p. 136.

65 Bill Bell, 'Fiction in the marketplace: towards a study of the Victorian serial', in Robin Myers and Michael Harris (eds), *Serials and Their Readers 1620–1914* (Winchester, St. Paul's Bibliographies; New Castle, DE: Oak Knoll Press, 1993), p. 136.

66 Norman Feltes, 'The moment of Pickwick, or the production of a commodity text', in Peter Humm, Paul Stigant and Peter Widdowson (eds), *Popular Fictions: Essays in Literature and History* (London, Methuen, 1986), p. 53; Feltes is quoting Karl Marx, *Capital* (Harmondsworth, Penguin, 1976), Vol. I, p. 1017.

Reading adaptations

NINETEEN THIRTY-FIVE SAW the appearance of James Whale's film *The Bride of Frankenstein* as a sequel to his enormously successful 1931 adaptation of Mary Shelley's *Frankenstein*, a film which established an image of the Monster that is still the dominant one within the contemporary popular imagination.[1] Whale opens his second *Frankenstein* film with a short prologue which takes the spectator, rather fancifully, to the site of the original novel's composition: Lord Byron, Percy and Mary Shelley are gathered together in the extremely Gothic Villa Diodati whilst a suitably violent storm rages in the world outside. In a scene which is, one has to assume, deliberately 'camp', the two men discuss Mary Shelley's original rendition of the *Frankenstein* story as a chilling fireside tale, expressing surprise that a tale of such horror should emerge from one so apparently innocent. Mary responds by reminding them (perhaps rather ambiguously) of the story's moral purpose and Byron continues by recalling in some detail the key moments of the original narrative. What is significant for the present discussion is the fashion in which Whale handles this retelling of the 'original' story. In the context of a sequel to Whale's adaptation of Shelley's novel, there are two 'originals' to which reference can be made. From the perspective of *The Bride of Frankenstein*, the 'original' narrative is both Shelley's novel and Whale's adaptation of it in that both provide, in effect, the point of departure for any sequel that is produced. Whale's decision to open his second film with the Villa Diodati sequence would seem to suggest that the 'original' is envisaged as Shelley's novel (or, at least, her oral tale which preceded publication). That this is not the case is revealed by the way in which Whale allows Byron to retell the 'original' story: as he casts his mind back, the scene shifts to a montage of clips from Whale's 1931 adaptation of *Frankenstein* which is accompanied by Byron's voiceover. The film thus playfully distorts the spectator's sense of the 'original' narrative in that the 'original' Mary Shelley story as 'told' by the character of Lord Byron turns out to be a version of Whale's own earlier film (constructed in such a way as to allow for the sequel that is to follow).

John Ellis has observed about film adaptations that the 'adaptation trades upon the memory of the novel, a memory that can derive from actual reading, or, as is more likely with a classic of literature, a generally circulated cultural memory. The adaptation consumes this memory, aiming to efface it with the presence of its own images.'[2] The opening scenes from *The Bride of Frankenstein* offer a clear example of this intention in practice in that the audience is asked to share the belief that Shelley's *Frankenstein* can successfully be replaced by a sequence of images from Whale's 'original' adaptation. Frankenstein, then, becomes Whale's rather than Shelley's fiction, but, more than this, the novel's author too becomes a fiction and is denied any autonomy outside of the text in which she is now made to appear. No longer the originator, 'Mary Shelley' becomes part of the commodity which is sold within the marketplace of popular culture, a process that is again evident in the more recent adaptation directed by Kenneth Branagh which, in its title, declares itself to be *Mary Shelley's Frankenstein*.[3] Such commodification and loss of authorial autonomy would indeed seem to represent a nightmarish fruition of the worst fears of both Scott and Dickens as revealed in the preceding chapters of the present book.

In light of this it is interesting to consider Mary Shelley's initial response to contemporary stage adaptations of her novel. Whilst she was in Paris in July 1823, William Godwin wrote to inform her that Richard Brinsley Peake's adaptation *Presumption, or the Fate of Frankenstein* was being performed very successfully in London; she writes to Leigh and Marianne Hunt in August that he 'does not know much English News, except that they brought out Frankenstein at the Lyceum and vivified the Monster in such a manner as caused the ladies to faint away & a hubbub to ensue –

however they diminished the horrors in the sequel, & it is having a run'.[4] Five years after the original publication of the novel, the monster has been brought back to life again, this time not by a misguided scientific genius (nor by a novelist with serious intellectual aspirations) but, it would seem, by a commercially inspired popular playwright who aspires to no more than simple Gothic thrills. It will be recalled that when Elizabeth Inchbald read William Godwin's *Caleb Williams* she noted how it combined sensations of pleasurable horror with the demands of intellectual rigour; Shelley's novel is similar in this respect to that of her father, but it is clear from the tone of the present letter that she expects *Presumption* to sacrifice the latter to the former. That this was the case is confirmed by her response to the play when she returned to London in August and had the opportunity to see it for herself:

> But lo & behold! I found myself famous! – Frankenstein has prodigious success as a drama & was about to be repeated for the 23rd night at the English opera house. The play bill amused me extremely, for in the list of dramatis personae came, —— by Mr T. Cooke: this nameless mode of naming the unnameable is rather good. On Friday Aug. 29th Jane My father William & I went to the theatre to see it. Wallack looked very well as F[rankenstein] – he is at the beginning full of hope & expectation – at the end of the 1st Act. the stage represents a room with a staircase leading to F workshop – he goes to it and you see his light at a small window, through which a frightened servant peeps, who runs off in terror when F. exclaims 'It lives!' – Presently F himself rushes in horror & trepidation from the room and while still expressing his agony & terror —— throws down the door of the laboratory, leaps the staircase & presents his unearthly & monstrous person on the stage. The story is not well managed – but Cooke played ——'s part extremely well – his seeking as it were for support – his trying to grasp at the sounds he heard – all indeed he does was well imagined & executed. I was much amused, & it appeared to excite a breathelss [*sic*] eagerness in the audience – it was a third piece a scanty pit filled at half price – & all stayed till it was over. They continue to play it even now.[5]

This is a very favourable response to the adaptation which responds positively to the acting and stagecraft of the theatre company. None the less, like Scott, who complained that the French operatic version of *Ivanhoe* 'mangled' the story of his novel, Shelley observes that in Peake's play the 'story is not well managed'. She also appears to differentiate her response to the play's Gothic horror from that of the audience. Whilst she records her own simple and rather dispassionate amusement at the spectacle before her, she notes that the rest of the theatre audience (for whom, presumably, such entertainment was more regular fare) responded with a far more involved 'breathless eagerness'. As is evidenced by her ironic appreciation of the play bill's use of '——' to designate the nameless monster, she approaches the whole performance as a good-natured joke, as something which should not be taken too seriously.[6]

However, at the same time, she is clearly aware that the existence of such a popular adaptation has had a marked effect upon her own social and cultural visibility: 'But lo & behold! I found myself famous!' At a time when she was struggling financially, this could have its advantages. Later in the same letter she records that her father has had a 'new edition' of *Frankenstein* published, for her 'benefit' on the 'strength of the drama'.[7] The popularity of the adaptation, it was hoped, could improve sales of the original novel: this situation perhaps appears very 'modern', but a similar argument was used in his own defence by William Moncrieff to Charles Dickens in 1837: 'Some apology is due to Mr Dickens, for the liberty taken with him, in finishing his work before its time; but the great increase in popularity, which it must have received, from my putting it upon the stage, will, I think, more than excuse a step, to which I was urged, rather by circumstance than desire.'[8] The 'popularity' of the adaptation could increase the popularity or fame of both the original novel and its author. And yet, paradoxically, as the case studies in the present book have shown, the popular adaptations were clearly and distinctly different kinds of texts from the novels (or verse narratives) upon which they were based. For them to bestow a secondary popularity on these original texts would be for those texts to be recreated to a significant extent in the image of their adaptations. In the case of Mary Shelley, the ultimate recreation of this kind is perhaps to be found in the opening scenes of *The Bride of Frankenstein* where she appears not as the author of *Frankenstein* but as a fictional account of herself as the author of a text that both is and is not her own.

If we follow Shelley's lead, it is tempting to see the adaptation itself as a '(re)vivified' monster, a monstrous doppelganger which offers a disturbing and uncontrollable 'other' to the original novel which effectively brought it into being. Such a model might be attractive when thinking about stage adaptations of the period as a whole and would certainly go some way towards providing a structure of explanation for, for example, the seemingly obsessive nature of Dickens's attacks upon Moncrieff. However, perhaps one should pay more detailed attention to the lessons to be learnt from Shelley's novel – particularly the fact that monstrosity is only present in the eyes of the beholder. If the monster and the adaptations are allowed to 'speak' for themselves (as, hopefully, they have been allowed to do in the present book) they will be found to have a far more engaging and humane voice which often possesses its own integrity and dignity. In his account of film adaptations of *Frankenstein*, Paul O'Flinn observes that there 'is no such thing as *Frankenstein*, there are only *Frankensteins*, as the text is ceaselessly rewritten, reproduced, refilmed and redesigned'.[9] Rather than seeing this in terms of what he calls 'a naive deconstructionist delight at the endless plurality of meanings the text has been able to afford', he proceeds to offer readings of both the original novel and its film adaptations in terms of the specific cultural and political conditions of their production and reception. He is thus able to provide a convincing account of the 'prodigious efforts made over the last century and a half to alter and realign the work and its meanings'. What the present study has aimed to demonstrate is that the contemporary popularity of stage adaptations of the works focused upon here means that from virtually the very outset it is necessary to talk of not one but several versions of *Caleb Williams* or *The Lady of the Lake* or *Ivanhoe* or *Pickwick Papers*. As has been seen, the generic shift occasioned by adaptation opened up the possibility for implicit and explicit debate about the ideological implications of the original work. In this way adaptations staged a lively and very public alteration and realignment of the works and their meanings in the context of a society undergoing enormous social, political, economic and cultural transformation.[10]

As long ago as 1958, Raymond Williams described the tortured and ambiguous attitude of the 'Romantic Artist' towards the increasingly powerful book-buying public which ultimately resulted in the rejection of the 'popular' both as a criterion of literary value and as the goal of the 'serious' writer.[11] The present book has not focused upon the unproblematically canonical poets discussed by Williams but rather upon writers from the same period who demonstrate a more ambivalent relationship with notions of popularity. To a significant extent, Godwin, Scott and Dickens court the very popularity that Wordsworth, Coleridge, Keats and Shelley rejected. In *Caleb Williams*, Godwin aimed to produce a 'popular' and therefore more accessible version of his philosophical musings upon political justice; Scott and Dickens, in their different ways, aimed to produce popular works which would further their aspirations as 'serious' professional writers. Contemporary reviews of Scott and Dickens in particular reveal the precarious nature of their undertaking: as the aesthetic criteria outlined in Williams's study of the 'Romantic Artist' were assimilated into a form of critical consensus, popularity was increasingly seen as antithetical to artistic worth. The presence of the stage adaptations served to magnify the tensions that were already implicit within the texts themselves. In this sense, in the eyes of Godwin, Scott and Dickens they must indeed at times have appeared as uncontrollable and monstrous 'others' brought into being by the ambitions for popularity inherent within their original narratives.

What is evident from the novels, poems and plays studied in the present book is that adaptations in reading practices during the Romantic period resulted in an increasingly clear dividing line between 'high' and 'low' culture within critical discourse. In his attack upon the 'high intellectual' criticism of John Forster, William Moncrieff demonstrated an astute awareness of the ways in which critical paradigms were being developed that would exclude his own artistic practice from serious critical attention. Viewing such issues from the late twentieth century, one would reject any critical strategy that denied literary merit on the grounds of a work's popularity, and yet it is still the case that late eighteenth- and early nineteenth-century stage adaptations – indeed, that period's dramatic works as a whole – are largely unknown and unread. In order to rediscover the rich diversity of the period, in order to appreciate its cultural range and depth, it behooves us in this respect to undertake our own contemporary reading adaptations.

Notes

1 Two useful essays on film adaptations of *Frankenstein* are Albert J. Lavelley, 'The stage and film children of *Frankenstein*' and William Nestrick, 'Coming to Life: *Frankenstein* and the nature of film narrative', both in George Levine and U. C. Knoeplfmacher (eds), *The Endurance of Frankenstein: Essays on Mary Shelley's Novel* (Berkeley, CA and London, University of California Press, 1979).

2 John Ellis, 'The literary adaptation: an introduction', *Screen*, 23/1 (May/June 1982) 3–5, p. 3.

3 *Mary Shelley's Frankenstein* (1994), directed by Kenneth Branagh, screenplay Steph Lady, starring Kenneth Branagh, Robert de Niro, Helena Bonham Carter.

4 Mary Shelley to Leigh and Marianne Hunt, 13 and Thursday 14 August 1923, in Shelley, *The Letters of Mary Wollstonecraft Shelley, Volume 1: 'A Part of the Elect'*, ed. Betty T. Bennett (Baltimore, MD and London, Johns Hopkins University Press, 1980), p. 369. For a useful discussion of Peake's *Presumption*, see Chris Baldick, *In Frankenstein's Shadow: Myth, Monstrosity, and Nineteenth-century Writing* (Oxford, Clarendon Press, 1987), pp. 58–60.

5 Mary Shelley to Leigh Hunt, 9 September 1823, Shelley, *Letters*, Vol. 1, p. 378.

6 Fred Botting interestingly comments upon the public outrage that the perceived morality of Peake's play often provoked ('crowds protested outside theatres, letters of complaint were written'); he suggests that Shelley's conservative reworking of the novel in 1831 was in part a response to her experience of the play: 'It was only after Mary Shelley had been exposed to the play ... that Frankenstein was constructed as a transgressor of a divinely sanctioned moral code: in the 1831 Introduction, the human creator is described as endeavouring to "mock the stupendous Creator of the world"', in *Making Monstrous: Frankenstein, Criticism, Theory* (Manchester, Manchester University Press, 1991), pp. 190–1. Whilst there is undoubtedly some truth in this hypothesis, it is clear that Shelley's initial reaction to the play itself was not one which revealed undue concern about its moral purpose or effect.

7 Mary Shelley to Leigh Hunt, 9 September 1823, Shelley, *Letters*, Vol. 1, p. 379.

8 Moncrieff, 'Advertisement' to *Sam Weller, or, the Pickwickians* (London, 1837), p. iv.

9 Paul O'Flinn, 'Production and reproduction: the case of *Frankenstein*', in Peter Humm, Paul Stigant and Peter Widdowson (eds), *Popular*

Fictions: Essays in Literature and History (London, Methuen, 1986), p. 197.

10 Deborah Vlock gestures twoards this broader cultural context in her discussion of Dickens: 'Dickens's readers actively participated in a creative-dramatic process, with the reading public itself a fertile field in which novel and theatre merged and became indistinguishable, thoroughly integrated into a larger fabric of ideas and desires', in *Dickens, Novel Reading, and the Victorian Popular Theatre*, Cambridge, Cambridge University Press, 1998) p. 79.

11 Raymond Williams, *Culture and Society 1780–1950* (Harmondsworth, Penguin, 1961; first published 1958), see Chapter 2, 'The romantic artist'.

Bibliography

Anon., *The Lady of the Lake: A Romance, in Two Volumes. Founded on the Poem so called by Walter Scott, Esq.*, London, Thomas Tegg, 1810.

Almar, G., *Oliver Twist. A Serio-Comic Burletta in Three Acts*, London, Chapman and Hall, 1838.

Backscheider, P. R., *Spectacular Politics: Theatrical Power and Mass Culture in Early Modern England*, Baltimore, MD and London, Johns Hopkins University Press, 1993.

Baillie, J., *The Complete Poetical Works of Joanna Baillie*, Philadelphia, PA, Carey and Lea, 1832.

——, *Miscellaneous Plays*, 2nd edn, London, Longman, Hurst, Rees, and Orme, 1805.

Baldick, C., *In Frankenstein's Shadow: Myth, Monstrosity, and Nineteenth-century Writing*, Oxford, Clarendon Press, 1987.

Ball, M., *Sir Walter Scott as a Critic of Literature*, Columbia University Press, 1907, reprinted, Port Washington, NY, Kennikat Press, 1966.

Barnett, C. Z., *Oliver Twist, or, The Parish Boy's Progress. A Domestic Drama, in Three Acts*, London, J. Duncombe, 1838.

Barreca, R., '"The mimic life of the theatre": The 1838 Adaptation of Oliver Twist', in C. H. Mackay (ed), *Dramatic Dickens*, London, Macmillan, 1989.

Bate, J., *Shakespearean Constitutions: Politics, Theatre, Criticism 1730–1830*, Oxford, Clarendon Press, 1989.

Bell, B., 'Fiction in the marketplace: towards a study of the Victorian serial', in Robin Myers and Michael Harris (eds), *Serials and Their Readers 1620–1914*, Winchester, St. Paul's Bibliographies; New Castle, DE, Oak Knoll Press, 1993.

Blake, R., *Disraeli*, London, Eyre and Spottiswoode, 1966.

Boaden, J., *Memoirs of Mrs Inchbald*, 2 volumes, London, Richard Bentley, 1833.

Bolton, H. P., *Dickens Dramatized*, London, Mansell Publishing, 1987.

——, *Scott Dramatized*, London and New York, Mansell Publishing, 1992.

Booth, M. R., 'Melodrama and the working class', in C. H. Mackay (ed.), *Dramatic Dickens*, London, Macmillan, 1989.

Booth, M. R., Southern, R., Marker, F and L.-L., and Davies, R., *The Revels History of Drama In English: Volume VI, 1750–1880*, London, Methuen, 1975.

Botting, F., *Making Monstrous: Frankenstein, Criticism, Theory*, Manchester, Manchester University Press, 1991.

Briggs, A., *The Age of Improvement 1783–1867*, London, Longman, 1959.

Brooks, P., *The Melodramatic Imagination: Balzac, Henry James, Melodrama, and the Mode of Excess*, New Haven, CT and London, Yale University Press, 1976.

Brown, F. K., *The Life of William Godwin*, London and Toronto, Dent; New York, Dutton, 1926.

Burwick, F., *Illusion and the Drama: Critical Theory of the Enlightenment and Romantic Era*, Pennsylvania, PA, Pennsylvania State University Press, 1991.

[Bury, C.], *The Exclusives*, 3rd edn, London, Colburn and Bentley, 1830.

Butler, M., 'Godwin, Burke and *Caleb Williams*', *Essays in Criticism*, 32 (1982) 237–57.

——, *Romantics, Rebels and Reactionaries: English Literature and its Background 1760–1830*, Oxford, Oxford University Press, 1981.

Carlson, J. A., *In the Theatre of Romanticism: Coleridge, Nationalism, Women*, Cambridge, Cambridge University Press, 1994.

Cave, R. A. (ed.), *The Romantic Theatre: An International Symposium*, Totowa, Barnes and Noble Books, 1986.

Chittick, K., *Dickens and the 1830s*, Cambridge, Cambridge University Press, 1990.

Clemit, P., *The Godwinian Novel: The Rational Fictions of Godwin, Brockden Brown, Mary Shelley*, Oxford, Clarendon Press, 1993.

Clery, E. J., *The Rise of Supernatural Fiction 1762–1800*, Cambridge, Cambridge University Press, 1995.

Coleridge. S. T., *Biographia Literaria or Biographical Sketches of My Life and Opinions*, ed. James Engel and W. Jackson Bate, 2 volumes, London, Routledge and Kegan Paul, 1983.

Collins, P. (ed.), *Dickens: The Critical Heritage*, London, Routledge, 1971.

Colman, G. (the Younger), *The Iron Chest*, in E. Inchbald (ed), *The British Theatre*, Vol. XXI, London, Longman, Hurst, Rees and Ormes, 1808.

Cox, J. N., 'Ideology and genre in the British anti-revolutionary drama of the 1790s', *ELH*, 58 (1991) 579–610.

—— (ed.), *Seven Gothic Dramas 1789–1825*, Athens, OH, Ohio University Press, 1992.

——, 'The Vision of Romantic Tragic Drama in England, France, and Germany', unpublished PhD thesis, University Of Virginia, 1981.

Cox, P., *Gender, Genre and the Romantic Poets*, Manchester, Manchester University Press, 1996.

——, '*Wuthering Heights* in 1939: novel, film and propaganda', *Bronte Society Transactions*, 20:5 (1992) 283–8.

Cronin, R., 'Carps and *Caleb Williams*', *Keats–Shelley Review*, 1 (Autumn 1986) 35–48.

Cross, N., *The Royal Literary Fund 1790–1918: An Introduction to the Fund's History and Archives with an Index of Applicants*, London, World Microfilm Publications, 1984.

Curran, S., *Poetic Form and British Romanticism*, New York and Oxford, Oxford University Press, 1986.

Dalziel, M., *Popular Fiction 100 Years Ago: An Unexplored Tract of Literary History*, London, Cohen and West, 1957.

[Dibdin, C.], *The Lady of the Lake. A Drama, in Three Acts; Founded on the Popular Poem written by W. Scott, Esq. Arranged as it is now performed, at the Theatre-Royal, Dublin. Revised from the Prompt Book, by Permission of the Manager*, Dublin, J. Charles, n.d.

Dibdin, T., *Ivanhoe; or, The Jew's Daughter; A Melo Dramatic Romance, in Three Acts. First Performed at the Surrey Theatre, on Thursday, January 20, 1820*, London, Roach, 1820.

Dickens, C., *Dickens's Journalism: Sketches By Boz and Other Early Papers 1833–39*, ed. Michael Slater, London, J. M. Dent, 1994.

——, *Nicholas Nickleby*, London, Penguin Popular Classics, 1994.

——, *The Pickwick Papers*, ed. Robert L. Patten, London, Penguin, 1972.

——, *The Pilgrim Edition of The Letters of Charles Dickens*, ed. Madeline House and Graham Storey, Oxford, Clarendon Press, 1965.

Donkin, E., *Getting into the Act: Women Playwrights in London 1776–1829*, London, Routledge, 1995.

Dubrow, H., *Genre, The Critical Idiom*, London and New York, Methuen, 1982.

Duncan, I., *Modern Romance and Transformations of the Novel: The Gothic, Scott, Dickens*, Cambridge, Cambridge University Press, 1992.

Egan, P., *Life in London; or, the Day and Night Scenes of Jerry Hawthorne, Esq., and his Elegant Friend Corinthian Tom, Accompanied by Bob Logic, the Oxonian, in their Rambles and Sprees Through the Metropolis*, London, Sherwood, Neeley and Jones, 1820–21.

Ellis, J., 'The literary adapatation: an introduction', *Screen*, 23:1 (May/June 1982) 3–5.

Eyre, E. J., *The Lady of the Lake: A Melo-Dramatic Romance, in Three Acts; Taken from the Popular Poem of that Title, And now Performing with undiminished applause, at the Theatre Royal, Edinburgh*, London, W. H. Wyatt, 1811.

Feltes, N., 'The moment of Pickwick, or the production of a commodity text', in Peter Humm, Paul Stigant, and Peter Widdowson (eds), *Popular Fictions: Essays in Literature and History*, London, Methuen, 1986.

Ferris, I. 'Re-positioning the novel: Waverley and the gender of fiction', *Studies in Romanticism*, 28 (Summer 1989) 291–301.

Fitz-Gerald, S. J. A., *Dickens and the Drama, Being an Account of Charles Dickens's Connections with the Stage and the Stage's Connection with Him ...* London, Chapman and Hall, 1910.

Ford, R., *Dramatisations of Scott's Novels: A Catalogue*, Oxford, Oxford Bibliographical Society, Bodleian Library, 1979.

Forster, J., *The Life of Charles Dickens*, London, Chapman and Hall, 1872.

Galt, J. (ed.), *The New British Theatre*, London, Henry Colburn, 1814.

Gash, N., *Reaction and Reconstruction: English Politics 1832–1852*, Oxford, Clarendon Press, 1965.

Gaull, M., *English Romanticism: The Human Context*, New York and London, W. W. Norton, 1988.

Gill, S., *William Wordsworth: A Life*, Oxford, Clarendon Press, 1989.

Glavin, J., *After Dickens: Reading, Adaptation and Performance*, Cambridge, Cambridge University Press, 1999.

Godwin, W., *Caleb Williams*, ed. David McCracken, Oxford, Oxford University Press, 1982.

——, *Enquiry Concerning Political Justice and Its Influence on Modern Morals and Happiness*, ed. Isaac Kramnick, Harmondsworth, Penguin, 1976.

——, 'Of history and romance', (ed. Michael Gamer), at http://www.english.upenn.edu/~mgamer/Romantic/godwin.history.html.

Gordon, I. A., *John Galt: The Life of a Writer*, Edinburgh, Oliver and Boyd, 1972.

Harris, T., 'Problematising popular culture', in Tim Harris (ed.), *Popular Culture in England, c. 1500–1850*, London, Macmillan, 1995.

Hayden, J. O., (ed.), *Scott: The Critical Heritage*, London, Routledge, 1970.

Hays, M. and Nikolopoulou, A. (eds), *Melodrama: The Cultural Emergence of a Genre*, New York, St. Martin's Press, 1996.

Hazlitt, W., *The Works of William Hazlitt*, ed. P. P. Howe, 21 volumes, London and Toronto, Dent, 1930–34.

Heller, J. R., *Coleridge, Lamb, Hazlitt, and the Reader of the Drama*, Columbia and London, University of Missouri Press, 1990.

Henderson, A. K., *Romantic Identities: Varieties of Subjectivity, 1774–1830*, Cambridge, Cambridge University Press, 1996.

Hoagwood, T. A. and Watkins, D. P. (eds), *British Romantic Drama: Historical and Critical Essays*, London, Associated University Presses, 1998.

Inchbald, E. (ed.), *The British Theatre: A Collection of Plays with Biographical and Critical Remarks by Mrs Inchbald*, 25 volumes, London, Longman, Hurst, Rees and Ormes, 1808.

Kelly, G., *The English Jacobin Novel 1780–1805*, Oxford, Clarendon Press, 1976.

Klancher, J. P., *The Making of English Reading Audiences, 1790–1832*, Wisconsin, WI, The University of Wisconsin Press, 1987.

Lacy, M. R., *The Maid of Judah; or, the Knights Templars: A Serious Opera, in Three Acts*, London, John Cumberland, [1829].

Lamb, C., *Lamb as Critic*, ed. Roy Park, London, Routledge and Kegan Paul, 1980.

Lavelley, A. J., 'The stage and film children of *Frankenstein*', in G. Levine and U. C. Knoeplfmacher (eds), *The Endurance of Frankenstein: Essays on Mary Shelley's Novel*, Berkeley, CA and London, University of California Press, 1979.

Leaver, K., 'Pursuing conversations: *Caleb Williams* and the romantic construction of the reader', *Studies in Romanticism*, 33 (Winter 1994) 589–610.

Lindenberger, H., *Opera: The Extravagant Art*, London and Ithaca, NY, Cornell University Press, 1984.

Lukacs, G., *The Historical Novel*, trans. Hannah and Stanley Mitchell, London, Merlin Press, 1962.

McGann, J. J., *The Romantic Ideology: A Critical Investigation*, Chicago, IL, University of Chicago Press, 1983.

——, 'Rethinking romanticism', *ELH*, 59 (1992) 735–54.

Mackay, C. H. (ed.), *Dramatic Dickens*, London, Macmillan, 1989.

Mandler, P., *Aristocratic Government in the Age of Reform: Whigs and Liberals, 1830–1852*, Oxford, Clarendon Press, 1990.

Manvell, R., *Elizabeth Inchbald: A Biographical Study*, Lantham, New York and London, University Press of America, 1987.

Millar, D. A., *The Novel and the Police*, (Berkeley, CA, University of California Press, 1988.

Moncrieff, W. T., *Ivanhoe! or, The Jewess. A Chivalric Play, in Three Acts; Founded on the Popular Romance of 'Ivanhoe'*, London, Lowndes and Marshall, 1820.

——, *The March of Intellect, A Comic Poem*, London, William Kidd and Charles Tilt, 1830.

——, *Poems*, Printed (For Private Distribution Only) at the Author's Private Address, Saville House, Lambeth, 1829.

——, *Sam Weller, or, the Pickwickians. A Drama, in Three Acts, As Performed at the New Strand Theatre, with Unexampled Success ...*, London, Published for the Author. And sold by all respectable Booksellers. 1837.

——, *Tom and Jerry; or, Life in London: An Operatic Extravaganza*, London, Richardson and Penny; Edinburgh, Hunter; Paris, Truchy, 1828.

Moretti, F., *The Way of the World: The Bildungsroman in European Culture*, London, Verso, 1987.

Morton, T., *The Knight of Snowdoun; A Musical Drama, in Three Acts, As it is performed at the Theatre Royal, Covent Garden*, London, Sharpe and Hailes, 1811.

Murphy, P., *Poetry as an Occupation and an Art in Britain 1760–1830*, Cambridge, Cambridge University Press, 1993.

Naman, A. A., *The Jew in the Victorian Novel: Some Relationships Bewteen Prejudice and Art*, New York, AMS Press, 1980.

Nestrick, W., 'Coming to life: *Frankenstein* and the nature of film narrative', in G. Levine and U. C. Knoeplfmacher (eds), *The Endurance of Frankenstein: Essays on Mary Shelley's Novel*, Berkeley, CA and London, University of California Press, 1979.

Nicoll, A., *A History of English Drama 1660–1900: Volume IV Early Nineteenth-Century Drama 1800–1850*, (Cambridge, Cambridge University Press, 1955)

Nikolopoulou, A., 'Historical disruptions: the Walter Scott melodramas', in Michael Hays and Anastasia Nikolopoulou (eds), *Melodrama: The Cultural Emergence of a Genre*, New York, St. Martins Press, 1996.

O'Flinn, P., 'Production and reproduction: the case of *Frankenstein*', in Peter Humm, Paul Stigant, and Peter Widdowson (eds), *Popular Fictions: Essays in Literature and History*, London, Methuen, 1986.

Patten, R. L., *Charles Dickens and His Publishers*, Oxford, Clarendon Press, 1978.

Pemberton, T. E., *Charles Dickens and the Stage*, London, George Redway, 1888.

Pocock, I., *Rob Roy Macgregor; or Auld Lang Syne! A Musical Drama in Three Acts*, London, Miller, 1818.

Purinton, M., *Romantic Ideology Unmasked: The Mentally Constructed Tyrannies in Dramas of William Wordsworth, Lord Byron, Percy Shelley, and Joanna Baillie*, Newark, DE, University of Delaware Press, 1994.

Ragussis, M., 'Writing nationalist history: England, the conversion of the Jews, and *Ivanhoe*', *ELH*, 60 (1993) 181–215.

Rede, W. L., *Peregrinations of Pickwick; A Drama, in Three Acts*, London, Strange, 1837.

Report from the Select Committee on Dramatic Literature: with The Minutes of Evidence. Ordered by the House of Commons to be Printed, 2 August 1832, Dublin, Irish University Press, 1968.

Richards, K. and Thomson, P. (eds), *Essays on Nineteenth-Century Theatre*, London, Methuen, 1971.

Robertson, F., *Legitimate Histories: Scott, Gothic, and the Authorities of Fiction*, Oxford, Clarendon Press, 1994.

Roper, D., *Reviewing Before the 'Edinburgh' 1788–1802*, London, Methuen, 1982.

Russell, G., *The Theatres of War: Performance, Politics and Society, 1793–1815*, Oxford, Clarendon Press, 1995.

St Clair, W., *The Godwins and the Shelleys: The Biography of a Family*, London, Faber and Faber, 1989.

[Scott, W.], *The Fortunes of Nigel. By the Author of 'Waverly, Kenilworth,' &c*, Edinburgh, Archibald Constable; London: Hurst, Robinson, 1822.

Scott, W., *The Lady of the Lake. A Poem*, 10th edn, Edinburgh, Longman, Hurst Rees, Orme and Brown, 1814.

——, *The Letters of Sir Walter Scott*, ed. H. J. C. Grierson, 12 volumes, London, Constable, 1932–37.

——, *Ivanhoe*, ed. Ian Duncan, Oxford, Oxford University Press, 1996.

——, *The Journal of Sir Walter Scott*, ed. W. E. K. Anderson, Oxford, Clarendon Press, 1972.

Shelley, M., *The Letters of Mary Wollstonecraft Shelley, Volume 1: 'A Part of the Elect'*, ed. Betty T. Bennett, Baltimore, MD and London, Johns Hopkins University Press, 1980.

Shepherd, S., 'Melodrama as avant-garde: enacting a new subjectivity', *Textual Practice*, 10:3 (1996) 507–22.

Shepherd, S. and Womack, P., *English Drama: A Cultural History*, Oxford, Blackwell, 1996.

Shiach, M., *Discourse on Popular Culture: Class, Gender and History in Cultural Analysis, 1730 to the Present*, London, Polity Press, 1989.

Siskin, S., *The Historicity of Romantic Discourse*, Oxford, Oxford University Press, 1988.

Smith, G., *Charles Dickens: A Literary Life*, London, Macmillan, 1996.

——, 'Dickens and adaptation: imagery in words and pictures', in Peter Reynolds (ed.), *Novel Images: Literature in Performance*. London, Routledge, 1993.

Soane, G., *The Hebrew. A Drama, In Five Acts, As Performed At the Theatre-Royal, Drury Lane*, London, John Lowndes, 1820.

Steig, M., *Dickens and Phiz*, Bloomington, IN and London, Indiana University Press, 1978.

Stephen, L. (ed.), *Dictionary of National Biography*, London: Smith, Elder, 1889.

Stirling, E., *The Fortunes of Smike, or a Sequel to Nicholas Nickleby*, London, Sherwood, Gilbert and Piper, n.d.

——, *Nicholas Nickleby, A Farce, In Two Acts*, London, Chapman and Hall, [1838].

——, *The Pickwick Club: or, The Age We Live In! A Burletta in Three Acts*, London, Duncombe, 1837.

Sullivan, G. A., '"A story to be hastily gobbled up": *Caleb Williams* and print culture', *Studies in Romanticism*, 28 (Fall 1993) 323–37.

Sutherland, J., *The Life of Walter Scott: A Critical Biography*, Oxford, Blackwell, 1995.

——, *Victorian Fiction: Writers, Publishers, Readers*, London, Macmillan, 1995.

Thomson, E. P., *The Making of the English Working Class*, rev. edn, Harmondsworth, Penguin, 1968.

Thomson, P., 'The early career of George Colman the Younger', in K. Richards and P. Thomson (eds), *Essays on Nineteenth-Century Theatre*, London, Methuen, 1971.

Todorov, T., *The Fantastic: A Structural Approach to Literary Genre*, trans. Richard Howard, Cleveland, OH, Case Western Reserve Press, 1973.

——, 'The typology of detective fiction', from *The Poetics of Prose*, trans. Richard Howard, Cornell University Press, 1977, in D. Lodge (ed.), *Modern Critical Theory: A Reader*, London, Longman, 1988.

Trumpener, K., 'National character, nationalist plots: national tale and historical novel in the age of Waverley, 1806–1830', *ELH*, 60 (1993) 685–731.

Vanden-Bossche, C. R., 'Culture and economy in Ivanhoe', *Nineteenth-Century Literature*, 42:1 (June 1987) 46–72.

Vernon, J., *Politics and the People: A Study in English Political Culture, c. 1815–1867*, (Cambridge, Cambridge University Press, 1993.

Vlock, D., *Dickens, Novel Reading, and the Victorian Popular Theatre*, Cambridge, Cambridge University Press, 1998.

Watkins, D. P., *A Materialist Critique of English Romantic Drama*, Gainesville, FL, University Press of Florida, 1993.

Webb, T., 'The romantic poet and the stage: a short, sad history', in R. A. Cave (ed.), *The Romantic Theatre: An International Symposium*, Totowa, Barnes and Noble Books, 1986.

White, H. A., *Sir Walter Scott's Novels on the Stage*, New Haven, CT, Yale University Press; Oxford, Oxford University Press, 1927.

Williams, R., *Culture and Society 1780–1950*, Harmondsworth, Penguin, 1961; first published 1958.

Wilson, A. N., *The Laird of Abbotsford: A View of Sir Walter Scott*, Oxford, Oxford University Press, 1980.

Wordsworth, W., *William Wordsworth*, ed. Stephen Gill, Oxford, Oxford University Press, 1984.

——, *William Wordsworth: The Poems*, 2 volumes, ed. John O. Hayden, Harmondsworth, Penguin, 1977.

——, *The Letters of William Wordsworth*, ed. Alan G. Hill, Oxford, Oxford University Press, 1984.

——, *Wordsworth's Literary Criticism*, ed. W. J. B. Owen, London and Boston, MA, Routledge and Kegan Paul, 1974.

Index